Disrupting Data Governance

A CALL TO ACTION

Laura B. Madsen, M.S.

Technics Publications

BASKING RIDGE, NEW JERSEY

2 Lindsley Road, Basking Ridge, NJ 07920 USA

https://www.TechnicsPub.com

Cover design by Lorena Molinari

Edited by Lauren McCafferty

First Edition

First Printing 2019

Copyright © 2019 Laura Madsen

ISBN, print ed.	9781634626538
ISBN, Kindle ed.	9781634626545
ISBN, PDF ed.	9781634626569

Library of Congress Control Number: 2019952193

To Karl.

Acknowledgments

Of all of the tasks that I have done in the data industry, data governance has honestly been my least favorite. Back in college – 1994, to be exact – the time came for me to declare a major. I had already been in college for a couple of years, but I took a break to see if I was interested in managing a clothing store (spoiler: I wasn't). It was technically my junior year and I was undeclared. Finally, they told me I had to pick a major, so I chose to major in one of the hardest classes I took: psychology. I had absolutely no interest in therapy or becoming a psychologist, but under the gun, I picked psychology because I remembered how difficult the final exam was. I guess I have a pattern of picking things that I find challenging and then I attempt to break them apart into tiny pieces so that I can understand them better. That same inclination led me to write this book on data governance. I just had to tackle one of the most difficult, multi-faceted and convoluted functions in data programs because it is without a doubt the thing that is stopping us from harvesting great insights from our data.

I have a lot of people to thank for this book because it took a lot of research and discussions. I interviewed friends and friends of friends and total strangers. I read and re-read books and articles all in the name of trying to find a better way forward. I'm proud

II • DATA GOVERNANCE

of the result but it wouldn't be much without this list of stellar professionals (listed in alphabetical order by last name) who were willing to share their time and talents with me:

- Chris Bergh
- Kevin Burns
- Will Davis
- Donna Fernandez
- Juliet Fox
- Evan Francen
- Claudia Imhoff
- Steve Johnson
- Jason Meszaros
- Tom Moore
- Kiran Mysore
- Dan Olson
- Neil Raden
- Serena Roberts
- Nathan Salmon
- Jada Sheetz
- Margaret Todora
- Joe Warbington

To my "street team", those people that read early versions and gave me feedback and helped me with marketing messages:

- Serena Roberts
- Karl Madsen
- Erik van der Velde

There were a million other casual conversations that I had with people, and a few that were completely "off the record." If you're reading this, I thank you for taking the time and for your trust in me. Finally, a posthumous note of gratitude to the incomparable David Hussman; we never talked about data governance, but he shaped these pages as if we had. David taught me a lot about agile, about leadership, and about priorities.

Just about anything to do with data, data programs, analytics or the trendy "AI" are hot topics. Organizations are desperately trying to use their data as a differentiator, but few actually achieve that level of maturity. Many of the barriers we place in our way are of our own making. From under-staffing to the politics of who owns the programs. But most impactful is the idea that the data is "wrong" or can't be trusted. Data "as-is" in our systems reflect back what is happening. The data is not right or wrong, it's just data. If you can be open to the idea that it is telling you something – alerting you to some misaligned process or bad context – then you're on your way to the analytics maturity that organizations need to successfully use the data. The one thing I've learned through this journey, data governance is the flip side of data democratization. You can't have one without the other.

Contents

Foreword

By Mike Capone, CEO of Qlik

I've always believed in the importance of data governance. That belief was forged early through various roles I held at ADP, where we worked daily with highly sensitive information regarding payroll, taxes and individual personally identifiable information (PII). It only grew during my time as COO at Medidata, where our whole business centered around clinical trial data that could directly impact lives. You don't live in those highly regulated worlds without knowing the importance of data governance.

As CEO of Qlik, every day I'm speaking with customers about their data strategy and needs. Regardless of industry, leaders are increasingly aware of the importance of data governance to their overall performance. For any company, once you get beyond the core product or service, it's the combination of their data and how their people use that data that makes or breaks success. And that's really what's at the core of the data governance conversation. How do you get these most fundamental and strategic elements of the business – data and people – aligned for maximum impact?

There's a handful of consistent macro themes driving the need for a fresh, new look at data governance.

- Data creation and availability – users know there's more data out there than ever before. They know the organization already has it, and are frustrated by it not being available to them. Old models of governance, based on backward looking monthly and quarterly reporting for the executive management, just doesn't fit today's enterprises.

- Competition – everyone has access to more data than ever. Making it available to more employees for better and faster decision-making at market speed is crucial. Governance needs to account for the changing nature of data (e.g. social media), and include processes to make that data appropriately accessible based on use case. This way employees can provide value add in areas like more accurate customer service, and react to competitive offerings in time to keep customers engaged.

- Same data, different departments – well run organizations want different departments talking the same language with data. It serves nobody to have sales, marketing, development and customer service looking at data around things like sales forecasts or churn through different lenses. Governance needs to account for different roles needing a greater (but appropriately controlled) level of access to shared common data sets.

- Executive Demand for Data-Driven Decisions –
  organization are sitting on what executives see as piles of
  unused data, and they are pushing to see that data
  democratized to drive outcomes. Governance models
  need to understand that all data should be made
  available at some point, and its role/responsibility/data
  literacy levels that can help shape a flexible and scalable
  policy set vs. a one size fits all approach.

Laura Madsen is a great advocate for data, and is uniquely
positioned to take you through these challenges and point the
way forward. As a former Qlik Luminary, she stands out as one
of the best and brightest data enthusiasts in our ecosystem. We
share a passion for data's ability to create a positive impact in
every aspect of our lives. In this book, Laura clearly outlines the
data governance challenges we all face in every industry, and how
to make data more accessible and available in a smarter and more
scalable way.

As Laura mentions in the very first chapter of this book – like
nature, users will find a way, in this case to the data. This
fundamental truth requires leaders to take a fresh look at their
data governance models and to be open to new approaches.
From technology selection, to training programs, to considering
emerging methodologies like DataOps to help align IT, data
admins and data users across the business, every element is ripe
for change regarding data governance. I firmly believe your

company's success depends on its data strategy, and a data strategy without a strong and flexible data governance component leads you away from success. You have the data – now's the time to have the modern data governance strategy to match.

Introduction

I really hate data governance. I have been responsible for it both as an employee and supported many efforts as a consultant. I always gave it my all and, at the time, felt it was some of my best work - yet it was always a burdensome experience. There was too much work, it was ill defined and seemingly destined for failure.

Let's consider a river as a metaphor for data and data governance; in its purest state, data is very much like a rushing river with jetties, rapids, and waterfalls. Step in the wrong spot and you will be sucked into a whitewash that will take your breath away. Governance was an attempt to control the rushing water, so we created a series of locks and dams. Your data stewards are out there; oar in hand, attempting to navigate the deluge. Their goal is to help you safely interact with your data. But even with all that in place, the amount of data and high demand for data can make it seem like a futile endeavor.

Said another way, if governance is a funnel, we have two ways to modify the flow:

1. Limit the size of the top at the funnel
2. Expand the size at the bottom of the funnel

In our analogy here, the top of the funnel is the data entering your data governance efforts. Limiting the size at the top of the funnel makes data governance owners feel like they have more control. The bottom of the funnel represents data your end-users will ultimately have access to; naturally, the bottom part of the funnel is already limited. By design, current data governance practices limit the output of data by requiring seemingly all data to be "governed" or "managed" before end users can use it. A few years ago, it became commonplace to modify governance practices to focus it on key attributes in your organization - I implemented this modification in my most recent role as a BI Director. We realized it's not feasible to expect a few people to fully vet and approve every piece of data in your organization's data universe. So, rather than opening up the bottom of the funnel, we closed the top and limited the responsibility of the data governance program to only the list of approved organizational metrics. This method definitely makes the ratio of data feel more palatable, but it does nothing to improve your user's access to data, and often creates pent up demand for data.

I have always defined data governance as critical to any analytics work. In my first book, "Healthcare Business Intelligence," I named it the most important tenet to a successful BI program. Yet, in my experience and in my heart of hearts, I knew very well that what we were doing was wrong. I'd rarely seen traditional data governance practices work end to end - so much of it focused on *controlling* data rather than *using* data. Many data governance programs focused too much on prevention and as a result, made it too difficult to get data to an end-user. As a result, the program would be designated a failure, or the business users would find ways around it; fueling pockets of shadow BI everywhere you look.

If you talk to anyone in just about any role in data, they will tell you that data governance is really important. Yet, if you ask the business people that are using the data, their responses are split. Everyone agrees that you must "govern" data, but to what degree varies dramatically. Governance is one of the keys to successful data management, yet there's a lack of shared definition - or worse, the definitions are so broad that it becomes the proverbial "other bucket" of data management. It's no wonder we can't get traction.

Demand for data has never been higher. Angst of data people has never been higher. So, what gives? I know from firsthand experience that even well informed and well-intentioned people can take data and do odd things with it (sum an average? Use a pie chart for intricate analysis? Use correlation and causation interchangeably). But here's the deal, how in the world will these same people make smarter choices or even get more comfortable asking about the data and what it implies if we don't actually *give* them the data? How did you learn while growing up? It wasn't by sitting quietly and waiting for a wave of knowledge to suddenly and magically hit you – this is no different. End-users must be allowed to get in there and roll up their sleeves. Right now we have a funnel that is both small at the top and small at the bottom, with frustrated users who are (for right or wrong) taking matters into their own hands to answer their questions with data, and last but not least irritated executive sponsors - and that isn't good!

War and trust

Many data professionals have war stories about the dumb things that people did with data. I have so many of them, I've lost count. So, the idea that we can govern "appropriate usage" seemed like a panacea or cure-all, and I was totally on board but would eventually come to a different realization.

I've experienced the consequences of end users making decisions with "bad data;" my prime directive was to ensure that our data was in great shape and only then release it to our users. One occasion, we scrambled to fix some "bad data," but it was too late, the trust had been broken. I was at the helm of the data ship and I felt responsible, but in hindsight, the "bad data" wasn't really to blame. I had made a promise that was impossible to keep, a setup for failure, even then.

You see, there is really no such thing as "clean data," not when we're talking about the accuracy of petabytes of data – it's just not feasible to guarantee its cleanliness. *Maybe* when we all had a few megabytes in our data warehouses, we could expect that level of confidence, but those days are gone forever. We are now faced with a tsunami of data, more than any human or teams of humans could control, but before we get to that, we need to take a look back at how we got here. It's critically important, when you consider a change of this magnitude, to first understand the variables that brought us to this moment in time so we can avoid repeating past mistakes.

The history of data governance

I have this scene in my head about the origin of data governance. Imagine a big conference room, large executive leather chairs and windows framing a metropolis - Mad Men-style. Inside on an average Tuesday, all of the CXOs and VPs got together for their quarterly sales review. Each holding dear "their" numbers, but they were all different numbers. Arguments ensued; papers strewn about as each executive argued their own rationale. Finally, one of them exclaimed, "we have to govern this thing!"

I've always loved doing a little research. I went in search of books, articles, blogs, and people from as far back as possible to understand how we got to where are today with data governance. There is an alarmingly high amount of misinformation about data governance. A quick Google search will demonstrate some of the challenges about how we define data governance and how it works. I sifted out the noise for you and interviewed a number of folks that I really trust to give you a brief and accurate history of data governance.

When you Google data governance you get some fascinating stuff. First, a definition from SearchDataManagement.com:

"Data governance (DG) is the overall management of the availability, usability, integrity, and security of data used in an enterprise. A sound data governance program includes a governing body or council, a defined set of procedures and a plan to execute those procedures."

That wasn't quite satisfactory to me, so I kept looking. Wikipedia offers:

"Data governance is a data management concept concerning the capability that enables an organization to ensure that high data quality exists throughout the complete lifecycle of the data. The key focus areas of data governance include availability, usability, consistency, data integrity and data security and includes establishing processes to ensure effective data management throughout the enterprise such as accountability for the adverse effects of poor data quality and ensuring that the data which an enterprise has can be used by the entire organization."

May 2019

To begin with, I interviewed Claudia Imhoff. If you have spent any time in data, specifically data warehousing and data modeling, this name will be familiar to you. For those that are not familiar, Claudia is literally one of the founders of what we now term the "data warehouse." Who else could be better to help us understand the evolution of data governance?

My first question to Claudia was "how did this all start?" The answer: with stewardship. "Data Stewardship was primarily a function to provide context to data, look for data quality issues and be a bridge between those techie people and the non-techie people." Claudia said, "The role was desperately needed, as it was born from the re-systemization of data as the volumes were growing, even in the late nineties."

Today, most data governance programs still have data stewards. The role is meant to help arrange and bring order to chaos. Generally speaking, Stewards are not full-time roles, and there is usually a limited number for people that can fill the role. But their job is a big one: To make sure that all data released is well defined and within the appropriate limits (i.e. range of max and min) based on a broadly accepted and well-socialized definition.

Data stewards were meant to help solidify the squishy. There was an intuitive sense that there were issues, but no one really knew what "bad" meant. Did it mean bad data? Were they concerned about bad decisions? It was all up in the air. The hope was that data stewards could help bring clarity and objectivity to the data analytic work going on throughout the organization. But even back then, the trouble was that there were no clear definitions of what it meant to be successful with stewardship or governance. Despite attempts to tie data governance projects to specific business functions, many of those efforts were one-time improvements. Time and time again, governance and stewardship would start and then sputter out, incapable of proving the value they provided to the organization.

Value and return on investment (ROI) have always been a challenge in the data world. While there may be the proverbial pot of gold under the data rainbow, many times it's just an illusion. Because data work can be tech-heavy, and the "tech" part of the work is easier to tangibly define, we tend to prematurely invest money in software. But without tightly tying that investment to real, long-term benefits related to our data, we lose out on the positive portion of that calculation. And it's not just about associating governance with a project that has identified and tangible benefits; it's about attaching it to improved understanding, better or faster decision-making. You can tie your technology investments to usage and that may help, but as history has shown time and again, it sputters out because it's a short-term value.

Larger software projects such as metadata management and master data management round out the "tech-heavy" aspect of data governance. Virtually none of these efforts provide value to your end-users. Data people (I included) will tell you that metadata, MDM, and policies and procedures are critical to a well-vetted data governance effort. Unfortunately, the people you are there to support, the people that need to use the data, couldn't care two cents about a policy and procedure document. If you can't tie what you are doing *right now* to a tangible business value, it is time to step back and ask yourself why you are doing it.

Most data governance efforts are still focused on control. Literally attempting to make sure that all the data are defined, correct, and have "high quality." Many programs attempt to ensure that the average business user can fully understand every aspect of the data and don't accidentally misinterpret it or make erroneous decisions. Neither of which is possible of course.

The idea that all data can be "correct" is not possible for many reasons. The data is too "messy." There aren't enough people in any organization to "clean" it. Average end users don't see enough data to know what types of questions to ask. Most data departments don't have the business context or the time or the tools to address the core issue. The core issue is so-called "bad data" and it is just a symptom of a broken or misaligned method or process that created the data. Our broken data governance processes aren't optimized to help the organization improve the processes that create the "bad data," the data quality or to use the data more effectively.

I'm not saying that we should just stop trying to do the right thing when it comes to data governance or data quality. What I am saying is we have to stop chasing our own tail with unattainable goals; we must accommodate for the possibility of error. We have to consider where it's best to put our limited resources to ensure that we can squeeze every possible piece of value out of our data. It's time to challenge some long-held beliefs about data governance, quality, and usage.

Organizational impact of governance

For as long as there have been data governance practices, we've had executive sponsors. Over the years, I've been lucky enough to work with many executives in this way and there's one thing they all have in common: they're executives. Other than that, it's a crapshoot. Some are so detailed oriented they can't let go of day-to-day operations. Others are so high-level you wonder what color the sky is in their world. I've had amazing executive sponsors, but honestly, I've had more than my fair share of terrible ones too. For far too long now the role of an executive sponsor for governance, or really any data related function, has been ill-defined. Yet we rely on them for support when those all-important doors close.

Whether your executive has supported a data governance function in the past or not, it's time to clearly define the role and expectations of the executive sponsor. Data is too important to any organization to have your sponsor flying blind in that executive boardroom (no one likes that). If they are, in fact, going to support the governance function, the first thing that has to change is their level of participation. It's a rare executive that understands data governance. Most know that governance is needed to get insights out of the data. But this "new" data governance we're proposing here requires a bit of backbone, a whole lot of patience, and a thorough understanding of the why.

It's easy to blame the too-busy executive for their failings in executive support. More often, the truth is that we have failed to clearly and consistently communicate the value and challenges associated with data governance in a way the executive can understand. Communication is a two-way street; your executive must be willing to put in a little effort, but you also have to consider your audience when presenting the challenges and opportunities.

Disrupting data governance

Data governance is broken. There is no way to make incremental changes to fix it. At the core of the issue, not just with governance but also with all of analytics, is the urgent need to provide commensurate value. Executives have (begrudgingly?) come to terms with the fact that data is an important asset to their organizations, but many of them have been burned by the current methods and processes associated with good data governance that they are apprehensive, and rightly so. The data people in most organizations have tried their best, often under intense scrutiny, to build data assets (warehouses) and processes to get data out to the masses. But these same data people are often met with frustrated end users, overly critical stakeholders, and in many cases, peers who are completely checked out or that just don't have the time or interest in becoming "data literate."

For a long time, data professionals have used the mantra (and many still do) that "business users just don't understand." I know I've used it often and even recently. Data professionals feel that it's their responsibility to protect end-users from the mess, but seeing the mess actually helps our business partners understand the challenge, and empathize with why the work takes so long, as well as why it's so important. Protecting our business partners from this reality means we have created our own little mess and it has come back to bite us. Data professionals often unintentionally convince their business partners that they can't understand our struggles, even though we *know* we need them to.

As a result, data teams create data literacy programs to help the average business user understand the data better. I literally had an executive look at me and say: "isn't that *your* job?" to understand the data and provide insights? His point was that he doesn't go out and hire "data people" or "analysts" so why should he expect them to understand and use the data the way that my team could?

We have a chasm of our own making; one that if we are not careful will kill the data industry as we know it. We are already seeing signs. Many of us watch our hard work get diminished because a business unit went out and bought a new piece of software that provided insights the team was looking for. Celebrations abound and then, in the proverbial awkward meeting, everyone turns to you with a look that says "see, it's not that hard." It's happening all the time because every product out there has a dashboard tool embedded in it now. The integration of the data is becoming less and less important because the data they see is *good enough* for what they need.

The "old" way of data governance is at the center of much of this lack of use. Our command-and-control approach to governance has - by design - shielded our users from seeing how much work it takes to get to a "clean" set of data. Rather than improving the process upstream, data teams are often put in the position of fixing data downstream. A position that any data quality person will tell you is untenable. We have too much data, too much demand, and nowhere near enough resources.

We find ourselves in a time when petabytes of data are created daily; when anyone can easily acquire a software tool with its own database; when answers are demanded in nanoseconds. The parochial idea of having everyone slow down long enough so we can define data and control its usage is nuts.

Between outputs and outcomes

The outputs from the old way of doing data governance were long lists of activities that led to nowhere, and the outcome was often missed. The good intentions of more usable data, safe data, or well-defined data got lost in the shuffle of activities that didn't clearly align with the way the average user thinks about or wants to use data.

Re-framing data governance around the concept of *using* data is a small but critically important semantic change. The intent of governance was always around "appropriate usage" but the world changed, and our processes didn't.

After doing a lot of research for this book and talking to a long list of experts, one theme kept coming back, over and over again: trust. I heard it in almost every interview I held. I'd write it down on my whiteboard then I'd erase it and go on to something else. I think I did that at least ten times before I could no longer ignore it: data governance is about trust. I don't think that's a surprise, but what it means is that we have been marching along with a list of outputs for data governance that have almost nothing to do with the one outcome that matters - the trust.

I am advocating for what I term "radical democratization of the data." It's time to get the data out there. In order to do that, data governance teams will have to re-evaluate what they do and recalibrate toward helping the organization adjust to the concept that there is no such thing as 100% accurate data. Radically democratizing access to data means that we have to trust each other. The data professionals have to recognize that the average end-user is just trying to get their job done. And the average end-user has to acknowledge that the data team can't conceivably address every data or business nuance, especially without the context.

But, WHY?

In Simon Sinek's seminal book "*Start with Why,*" he laments that most people assume they know, but maybe they really don't, or if they do know they at least assume others know too. I think this is what has happened in data governance. We assumed that everyone knew why, and we lost our way. As a result, data governance could never really gain traction because we defined it as a what, not a why.

Why are we doing data governance? What value does data governance provide the business? If we can't prove without a reasonable doubt that what we are doing is providing value, we should stop doing it. There's too much other work to do to justify working on things that don't provide value to the business.

I break the "Why" of data governance into four functions:

Function	% of importance	Value
Increasing usage in assets	50%	Information to use
Quality (Context)	25%	Trust/Transparency
Lineage/Data Catalog	15%	Visibility
Protection	10%	Avoidance of risk

Under our new allocation of value, the protection of the data is ascribed only ten percent of importance. Why? Because protection is part of the broader effort of governance more appropriately placed with your security team. It is an effort that requires capabilities well beyond a typical data steward. It also, unfortunately, carries little weight with someone when they want to see data. It's like insurance; you only realize how much you really need after something bad has happened. We can't completely dismiss protection, but it should not be the thing that leads. The more important function, without a doubt, is the need to increase the usage of the data assets.

Besides the need to get more people in the data, and the re-alignment of protection to the InfoSec team, correctness can't be the goal either. The idea that the data is "correct" was something that most traditional data governance efforts rallied around.

When you put too much focus on correctness you lose room for nuances in the data. You may be introducing a bias that looks like a pattern. Just like the idea that a nurse manager and a finance manager define a patient differently, only having one way of defining and controlling your data may very well be impeding insights rather than supporting them. Here's a great example. Let's say a steward decides that all reports would only show patient counts during "business days," and the definition of business day was Monday through Friday. Unbeknownst to you or the steward, a clinic opens up for urgent care hours on Saturdays. The reports aren't modified, and as such, decisions are made from data that isn't shown. Technically the data is "correct" based on our own definitions. The goal of correctness implies a sense of all-knowing which is not scalable in a modern, fast-changing organization.

Being wrong isn't our problem, expecting to be right is. The truth is, particularly in the data world, correctness is an exercise in futility. When we seek first to be correct, we are saying we value consistency of the answer over the accuracy of the answer. That can lead to feeling the need to hide data, change the data or outright ignore data that doesn't fit into our version of correct. I've seen each of these scenarios play out in organizations that were absolutely trying their best. It's a slippery slope that leads to consistent bias, not accuracy. We are formulaically ignoring insights in pursuit of being right. The fact that the data wasn't entered correctly from the beginning is an insight in and of itself.

Instead, we chalk it up to a training problem or a difficult employee and move on. We are right, or are we?

If command and control can't be the goal and correctness can't be the goal, what the heck is the goal, you ask? Quite literally…messing up, "Failing fast" or whatever you want to call it. It's time to re-arrange your success metrics around usage and not the count of metrics released (or reports being used). Success should be end-users asking questions about data, success should be a ten-fold increase in your user base. Forget control - train your stewards on how to respond to questions and challenges and what to do when failures occur. Re-organize the concept of stewardship from preventing "mistakes" to responding when users have questions. Your stewards are like first responders for data, on the ground and ready to help.

How this book will help

You've got this far, so you are probably of a shared mindset or at least what I've said has resonated with you. In the following chapters, we will breakdown the shift in data governance to four familiar pillars: People, Process, Technology, and Culture. Each will be chapters that will outline the changes needed. In the "People" chapter we will revisit the job descriptions of the data governance roles, allowing for them to be assigned both to a specific function (i.e. finance) as well as keeping an "at-large" function. In the "Process" chapter we will see how data governance can adapt to agile methods and DataOps procedures to not only protect the sensitive data, but also promote usage. In the "Technology" chapter, we will learn how technology solutions must be a means to an end. In chapter five, "Culture," we will see how critical the concept of governance becomes when we reconsider the implications of the change. A data quality chapter will fill in some details that are critical for us to implement data governance into a modern data warehouse. Finally, we will put it all together and see the benefits of the disruption. This final chapter will be a framework to operationalize the change in your organization; full of checklists and backlogs for use in getting started toward a radical democratization of your organization's data.

Nothing is perfect and the more we try to make it perfect the faster we lose ground. Let's embrace the vulnerabilities; only then will we be able to improve the state of our data.

Before we start

As I was preparing to write this book, I interviewed a lot of people (find the list of interviewees in the acknowledgments section). Some are quoted directly while others provided a deeper contribution to the content, with no specific quotes. I learned so much from these individuals and will be forever grateful to them. One particular discussion prompted a small drawing on my whiteboard; I think it's important enough to acknowledge before we get too far. Joe Warbington was the Healthcare Analytics Director at a-large Data Visualization Company. I've known Joe for a few years now and he is a prolific content creator for both data visualization and the healthcare industry. He's seen a lot of companies and he knows what works and what doesn't. As he was talking, he referenced how impatient some companies were, and that the relative maturity of the organization in the data industry was an indicator of how much time data governance efforts really take.

A light went on in my head as I drew the axis for a line graph. I labeled the Y-axis "Time" and the X-axis "Maturity":

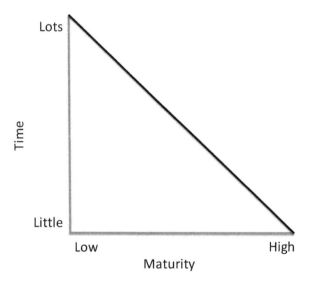

Take a minute to consider your organization's maturity with data. There are formal ways to measure this of course and we will cover them later. For now, as you sit there reading, just doing a quick gut-check: how mature is your organization with data? If you feel like you're on the low end of the maturity axis, just know that it will take you longer to find your footing. The part that no one wants to talk about is the value of the experience as you build any data governance effort; the effort and focus it takes to become more data mature is a benefit in and of itself. You learn, grow, hire differently and talk differently about what data means to the organization. Don't skip the work, because within the work is value and education. So even if you think you're "immature," embrace it and work to improve it. Just remember, it's going to take some time. Are you ready? Let's go!

CHAPTER 1

People

Want to learn something so completely radical and new that it will change your way of thinking forever? The only reason we do data governance is so people can actually **use the data**. This chapter is meant to be a wake-up call for anyone who finds themselves supporting or running a data governance function the "old-fashioned" way. Here it is: it's not about the technology; it's all about the *people*. I'm talking about the people who work with the data, the people who protect the data, and the people who use the data.

In all my years, I've never seen an appropriately staffed data governance effort. I've seen lots of well-staffed data quality efforts, but even those were often project-based and too narrowly scoped to make a real impact. We need to stop making data governance about technology, specific projects or the pursuit of perfect data.

It's true that not all people are created equal when it comes to data skills. Everyone is out there looking for a unicorn or a rhino (apparently a slightly more reasonable alternative to the unicorn?) You don't need to traverse the universe or go on safari in search of these mythical creatures. What you do need are smart, dedicated people and an open approach designed to democratize access to your data. Because if using your data isn't your primary goal, then what the heck are you doing?

This new evolution of data governance requires staffing, but not of the mammoth proportions the old data governance would have required if sourced appropriately; it requires smart and adaptive resources. In this chapter, we will cover the roles that are needed, the recommended number of people for each of those roles, and where those people should report to in the organization.

Let's talk about stewardship

Data stewards have been at the heart of most data governance efforts for the past few decades. They are the people that know the data and the source systems well. They speak the language of IT (because they have to be able to read data models) and translate that back to the business. The role requires the patience of a kindergarten teacher and the ability to successfully negotiate a hostage situation. Good data stewards aren't mythical creatures, but they are exceedingly rare, and *that's* why relying so heavily on them doesn't work.

According to Merriam Webster, stewardship is defined as the "careful and responsible management of something." Instead of a data steward, I like the idea of a data Sherpa, someone there to guide you through the complications that arise with the management of data. This person's goal should be to utilize the smart people around them that know the data and how people want to use it. Most importantly, the Sherpa is completely open to the notion that when people use data, they may screw up and that's just part of the process.

When I interviewed others about this idea; that we must let users make mistakes, there was a lot of nervousness. When pressed, the nervousness seemed to spring from a place of deep concern over regulations, privacy, compliance and risk avoidance. This actually is how a lot of data governance efforts get supported in organizations, through a risk control construct - we have to govern the data so we can control our risk. The focus of traditional data governance initiatives has always been the concept of control and protection.

How exactly does one control both the usage of an asset, while at the same time garner vast insights? Well, I think the truth is, you don't. Organizations that have taken a very traditional command-and-control stance with governance struggle to put their data to good use, while organizations taking a more liberal approach are finding insights faster than they can apply them.

Everyone seems to know they have to do data governance, but it has become the proverbial "other" bucket for data management. If there's an issue with the data, it's a governance issue. If someone doesn't understand the data, it's a governance issue. If there's not enough or too much data, it's a governance issue. We place the enormous responsibilities and pressures of access management, security controls, large work efforts like data classification matrices, and policy and procedure documentation onto data governance. Even when we succeed in these areas, we've provided little to no benefit to the people who actually use the data. Lost somewhere in the myriad of data governance responsibilities is the one thing that can save it...people using the data. I fully acknowledge that we have to protect the data, I just happen to believe accountability for that effort should fall squarely on your information security department. Data governance should be accountable for the promotion of the data asset, while only participating in the protection of the asset.

Ambassadorship makes a lot of sense for data governance. The function of an ambassador is to represent the highest rank of their country as they seek to protect and promote the interests of their leadership. The function of governance should be to balance the protection of data with the promotion of data while representing leadership interests. If no one is using your data, I suppose you've succeeded in protecting it; but I'm reasonably sure that your business partners who are financially supporting the effort, would not be singing your praises.

The tightrope of governance

Balancing the opposing forces of protection and promotion will take some effort, each needs to be well defined and managed to avoid losing focus on their respective goals. Continued support for data governance will require the ability to claim enough of a benefit to achieve a return on investment (ROI). The balance of promotion as well as protection is critical to long-term support. Without this yin and yang, you will always struggle to realize the benefits or justify an ROI, which is the sad state many organizations find themselves in now with data governance. What you will protect must be negotiated with your information security team. These groups vary in size between organizations and industries. The biggest shift you'll need to make if you're doing traditional data governance today, is this: you will have to become the subject matter expert for your InfoSec group.

I like using "RACI" models when dealing with large teams that have lots of moving parts. It clearly aligns with each role what the function is without having to do a deep dive into job descriptions. Here's how I see the RACI model for modern data governance playing out with InfoSec teams:

Function	Governance	InfoSec	Data Analysts
Policies & Procedures	C, I	R, A	C, I
Access Management	C, I	R, A	I
Data Classification	R	A	C, I

R = Responsible, A = Accountable, C = Consulted, I = Informed

Did I just blow your mind? If you've been in data governance long enough, the shift I'm proposing in the table above probably prompted you to mark the page and put down the book for a minute. I promise I have not completely lost my mind, so I ask you to trust me and allow me to explain in more detail.

The protection of data in the modern age has well outstripped the abilities of most data governance efforts; we haven't been hiring InfoSec professionals to these teams, and we never should. But programs like GDPR, recent legislation in California and to a lesser degree HIPAA and SOX, have put so many demands on the regulatory protection of the data that it requires a specialized skill set. If you force your data governance roles to be accountable for the implementation of these expansive security efforts, there is no way that they can also support the usage of the data - they will be too busy controlling the data. More importantly, protection and promotion are two different things. It's unreasonable to expect someone to successfully focus on both keeping data in *and* letting data out. It's better to have an InfoSec group you can partner with. They should take the lead on implementing security protocols, access management and providing requirements for data management teams. While the governance team is responsible for promoting the data assets and serving as a subject matter expert back to the InfoSec team. Your governance team should always have a dotted line to your InfoSec team while reporting directly to your Chief Data Officer.

Active versus passive management

Active management of the data is what stewards have historically been taxed with for the majority of their role. Whether for a project or a larger program effort, they were responsible for actively defining data, understanding the data itself, and helping both the technical people and the businesspeople toward appropriate usage of the data. It's a very full job and a "proactive" one in the management of the data. As data warehouses grew, the ability to scale toward active management of all of the data by a steward, or even a team of stewards, quickly became cruel and unusual punishment. On top of that, often the guidance provided by the stewards was never actually implemented into the data warehouse, typically because the technical team wasn't really sure what to do with it.

This is one of the reasons I hate data governance. The work was technically successful because it was based on the terms at the time, for example, we defined our key performance indicators. However, there was always disconnectedness between the process (complete definitions) and the technology (i.e. doing anything with those definitions). Let's not even talk about the fact that forcing the use of one definition for most organizations is not that feasible. I see three main gaps:

1. The gap between the technical team and the stewards, resulting in a failure to operationalize the good work of the steward.

2. The gap between the business people and the stewards, in (mis)alignment of purpose.

3. Finally, between the users and the stewards when the definitions didn't meet everyone's very specific perspective.

It became a blame game. The best you could hope for was good communication, which frankly was probably all we had the right to hope for in the first place.

Historically leaders and sponsors sat back and waited, they waited for the people responsible for data governance to bring them something they could respond to. As a good data professional, I always tried to limit the interaction the executives had with the data because I didn't want to burden them. But recently, as I've reflected on the successful and unsuccessful attempts I've had, I realized something. If data is the new oil or the lifeblood of an organization, why are we giving the execs a free pass? Would you ever expect your finance team to go rogue and come to you a year later and say, "oops we went bankrupt because we weren't sure where you wanted us to focus?" Yet we allow it to happen with this all-important "asset" all the time!

A switcheroo

In the past, the active roles were the stewards and analysts that lived and breathed in the data. The passive roles tended to be leadership, who would pass off the responsibility to lower levels of the organization. My proposal is to switch these active/passive roles. The leaders and sponsors should take an active role and the stewards and analysts should take a more passive role. Now I don't mean that the leaders and sponsors will facilitate sessions to determine the business definitions of data. What I do mean is that they are responsible for the success criteria and risk assessment of the data governance program. They *must* play an active role in understanding that actually using the data (which will drive ROI) introduces risk. The reward of more people in the organization using the data has to be worth the risk and only the people leading the strategy of the organization can make that determination.

Here's how this plays out. Someone as high up as possible in the organization has determined that you have to reframe your data governance effort because it's not working (or maybe you never had one to begin with). The first thing that happens is you have to re-establish the leadership functions of data governance. If this is coming from the executives, then they will have to decide if the current leader is effective. Obviously, if there isn't a current leader, then one must be selected or hired. Then the executive(s) and the leader must sit down and negotiate the terms of the new data governance function. The terms of this negotiation must cover these items:

- Scope
- Budget
- Success metrics
- Staffing
- Risk assessment

Part of the success of this new way of thinking about data governance requires that the leaders of the organization take an active, early role in creating the standards for success. If you want to use data and you need to find a way to make it valuable, it's incumbent upon the leaders of the organization to help frame that for the people that work in the data.

Scope

The key executive sponsor together with the data governance leader must decide what areas data governance will be responsible for and just as important, which areas you are *not* responsible for. The more specific you can be in this area the better off you are. It's not acceptable to just say something like "Data Governance will guarantee high-quality data" or "Data governance will govern all data." That's not winnable, that's a setup for failure. Areas of focus should be key organizational metrics, data usage metrics, data quality dashboards, improved data transparency, etc.

Budget

This will cost money; you can't reframe your data governance goals around usage without investing in it. If the organization doesn't want to invest in data governance, don't do it, and certainly don't try to do it and put someone in an untenable position. There will likely be some investment in technology, although most of the costs and efforts associated with data governance should be focused on the people and process, and less on the technology. That said, there are great technology tools that can help once you figure out what you want to do. This would also be a good opportunity to determine if you need some consulting support. Getting these programs up and running can take a significant amount of effort; additional support while you're laying the groundwork may be advantageous.

Success metrics

Imagine for a moment you are the new data governance leader. You're in the room with a couple of executives who've taken the time to make sure you get started on the right foot. You've come to terms with the scope and budget and you are feeling, for the first time, that this might actually work. Then a thought occurs to you, "What does done look like?" How will we know if the program is successful? Sure, you'll track your scope and spend your budget, but how will these executives know you actually did what you said you would? Now is the time, while you have them in the room with you, to determine a few success metrics for the program. They should be reasonable, objective and of course, you need to be able to track them. I like having a mix of data-specific ones (such as finalized algorithms or finalized definitions) and hospitality-based ones (such as satisfaction or ease of effort). Again, specificity is the key, but you can always go back to the executive sponsor with the definitions of things like "finalized" or what it means to "make it easy" to interact with data governance efforts.

Staffing

You will need people. Sure, some will likely be contractors or consultants helping with the build phase, but you can't do this without appropriate staffing. If I could put my finger on why most governance efforts fail, it would be because organizations tend to think that the work is done when they are done defining it. In reality, the work is never done, but what we can do is automate it as much as possible. That's why building it is a bigger effort, (or should be), than maintaining it. You will need to agree on headcount; I would start small because you don't want hiring, on-boarding and people management to slow you down. Hire a few key resources and get out of their way. Later in this chapter, I will identify those key resources.

Risk assessment

Scope, budget, success metrics and staffing seem pretty straightforward. You get to risk assessment and you're probably thinking: "I'll for sure do the other ones, but I'm not going to do a risk assessment with my executives." It just feels outside of the core of what data governance should do. The whole reason we even attempt to do data governance is because of risk; the risk of not managing the data, having different definitions, inadvertent disclosures, inappropriate usage. Take the time early in this process to identify what your executives are willing to put up with in terms of risk. You can find some risk assessment templates on my website at www.routetwentyfive.com.

Most projects have a risk log. It's one of the tools that I find really valuable. So, take a few moments and document all the areas in data governance where you have highlighted potential issues and risks. You will likely have a number of those already because you talked through your scope, budget, staffing, and success metrics. Write all of those down and describe them thoroughly, then create a method of determining probability and impact. Finally, define mitigation plans for those that exceed an agreed-upon threshold. It will be worth your time to find out where your executives are most concerned.

It can't end here. You must actively continue to interact with and include the executive sponsors in the program. Leaving them out just gives them time to forget and puts the leader in a position to have to re-explain and eventually defend their position. The first step is to create a shared understanding and approach to the work of data governance. The real effort to communicate with your executive sponsor comes as you build and automate.

Leading

First, let's make it clear that there is a difference between leadership and sponsorship. As active as we need our executive sponsors to be, they cannot be involved in the day-to-day; that's the leader's job. The executive sponsors can help us frame what we should be spending our time on, but the leader of the data governance function must be willing and able to steer the ship.

I have recently seen an influx of "Chief Data Governance Officers" and the like. Honestly, there's a glut of "Chief X

Officers" so I guess it shouldn't surprise me. I feel as strongly as anyone that data governance needs to be led and paid attention to, but not all roles require a chief. In many cases, including this one, it makes more sense to have a leader with the appropriate organizational authority to get the work done. In the past, data governance leaders were often individual contributors, buried deep within a team or department; warning: if you don't have the ability to influence upward or lack effective Executive Sponsorship, you're not set up for success.

Any data governance leader, regardless of what you call them, first needs to be an excellent communicator. Honestly, I would take an excellent communicator any day over a brilliant analyst. The trouble with analysts (not all, I am generalizing for the purpose of demonstration) is they are almost too detail-oriented and often have too much skin in the game. They have their own feelings about the data, the definitions, and how things should be used. That's one of the biggest issues with getting traction in analytics programs because the analysts have too much riding on being right.

The leader of your data governance effort should absolutely understand the data, and likely have a background in analytics or data modeling. This will give them a good framework to be able to talk with technical resources. But ideally, they have just as much, if not more, business experience - and in order to be truly successful, they must be able to talk the talk with the business. In the world of analytics, we're talking about the mythical data unicorn. When your search is a bust, find a horse you trust, get one of those unicorn headbands and empower them to be the unicorn you need.

Depending on the size of your organization and/or your willingness to fund data governance, you may need more than one person to lead the governance effort. There are a couple of different ways you can split the work, either by function (i.e. finance, operations, etc.) or just based on project intake. They should all report to a common person, ideally the head of your analytics function.

Up to this point, all these roles reside on the business side, or at least they *should*. Now we need to consider the data quality portion of the effort. There is no data quality without governance and no governance without data quality – two sides of the same coin. Data quality operations should be made up of quality assurance professionals that have experience in data, specifically data profiling. There are lots of quality assurance professionals that specialize in software, but that is not what we are talking about here. You need people that have experience analyzing data for inconsistencies and other anomalies, data cleansing activities that allow the team to flag and log issues to review and modify processes. Again, depending on the size of your organization and your willingness to fund this effort, you could have anywhere from two to ten people working in just your data quality operations. In a later chapter, we will dive deeper into these roles and discuss how they ensure "good" data quality, as well as transparency of the function.

Leading this new way of thinking about data governance won't be easy. You are forging new paths, helping your organization pioneer new ways to think about using data. Your challenge will be accompanied by distrust, discomfort and a Texas-size amount of ambiguity. Lots of people will push back. You will find people going off and doing their own thing. More often than not, you will find you and your team wanting to slide back to what feels comfortable, what you know.

When you find yourself at this point, and you're not sure what to do next, I want you to pause for a minute and resist the urge to "do something." Focus your efforts on the right kind of change; don't dilute the work by change for change's sake. Cut yourself some slack and recognize the gravity of the work you're doing. Give yourself some credit because leading through disruptive change is exceedingly difficult. If you really feel like something needs to change, start asking around. Ask your business stakeholders, the data quality operations folks, and your other data governance leaders. Then have a conversation with your executive sponsor. Don't get caught in the trap that if a change is disruptive it is therefore beneficial; sometimes change is just disruptive and a distraction to your team.

Update your job descriptions

There are a lot of job descriptions available on the Internet for data governance roles. Many of them use the word "control" a lot. Since we are re-framing data governance as ambassadorship, we will need to re-write all the job descriptions. Below is the one I created for the new "Data Ambassador" role. Feel free to use it or edit it for your purposes. I would also encourage you to review any of your job descriptions that involve data or governance to ensure the focus is on the usage of the data, or in terms of ambassadorship to "protect and promote."

Data Ambassador Job Description

The Data Ambassador will serve as a liaison between all business stakeholders, end-users and technical resources to protect and promote data assets. This highly influential role will interact with all levels of the organization, guide the development of data assets, and ensure usage of data assets to drive a positive value proposition.

Responsibilities

- Protect and promote all data assets
- Serve as the primary point of contact between disparate teams
- Provide support to the data team(s) in the development of new data assets and the enhancement of existing data assets

- Document appropriate data use policies and procedures in partnership with the organization's privacy and security officers
- Act as a subject matter expert to the organization's data quality team
- Support all users as they learn data
- Document and maintain risk assessment with executive data ambassador

Required Qualifications

- A minimum of five years' experience in a data-specific role
- Experience with data quality teams
- Capability to read data models and interact with data architects
- Excellent verbal and written communication
- A passion for helping the organization use data
- Experience with Agile methods
- Unicorns need not apply

Organizational alignment

A slight aside, but a relevant discussion point is where these functions should report to in the organization. I have always believed, and continue to believe, that you need a business leader that is directly responsible for the data program. Unfortunately, confusion exists because there is a lot about a data program that feels very technical. Don't get me wrong, there will be some people on your team that have deep technical skill sets, like database administrators and ETL engineers. But those roles wouldn't exist without the need to use data in the business. The split between IT and business has always been a symptom of an organization attempting to neatly categorize the functions. An organization that truly wants to have a data program that delivers value will employ an executive-level resource to lead the data programs and that individual would report to the highest level in the organization. In other words, they will have either a "Chief Analytics Officer" or a "Chief Data Officer" and that role will report into either the CEO or the COO. Instead of reporting to the CIO or CFO, they would be their peers. This is a critically important shift in how the organization uses data. If we think of data as a corporate asset, like technology or the financial operations, then source it like that. If you're willing and able, I highly recommend moving forward with a shared executive leader that has the ability to merge these historically disparate functions together.

A less appealing alternative, but one that (in reality) will be more adopted, is the disparate organization that is a matrix of business and IT. In this case, the data quality operations team will likely stay in IT and the data governance leaders will report to the business side. It's not ideal, as it requires an enormous amount of effort just to stay aligned, but some find it a more palatable organizational shift. The second these two groups are out of sync the effort spins off like a gyroscope without an axis. Be prepared to spend the time and energy keeping all of the associated leaders in lockstep, which can be a distraction from the actual work.

Wrapping it up

The executive sponsor role has to change from a passive "I only get involved when stuff goes wrong" to an active role; defining the function and staying in tune with the effort. In small organizations that are just starting this work, you can get away with two resources: a data governance leader and a data quality resource. Regardless of the size of the organization, you will need both sides of that coin. Out of all the recommendations in this chapter, the one I want you to keep in mind is this one: *there is no governance without quality and there is no quality without governance.*

CHAPTER 2

Process

I was fortunate enough to learn the fundamentals of agile from the venerable David Hussman. David was an institution in the agile community in the Twin Cities. He also worked tirelessly all over the world helping organizations and individuals better understand what the agile framework could do for them. He could weave together the agile concepts with a unique storytelling style that left me both exhilarated and exhausted at the same time. His insights were so prolific, I often found myself wishing for a real-life pause button to process them to the extent they deserved. David left an indelible mark on me. It's difficult to condense what I learned from David in just a few words, but what resonated with me the most was the idea that there is *no inherent value in the process.* You don't get points for checking a box or jumping through flaming hoops. The work and what you build are what matter. Why do we spend so much time creating a process around the work?

Too many organizations spend too much time creating difficult to follow processes, often with corresponding software, to prove that they are working. These convoluted processes are nothing more than a method for management and stakeholders to "check-in" on the people that are doing the work. Much of what is done, particularly in the IT space, takes time and feels abstract to people outside of IT. To create a sense of control and transparency, we identify all these steps and processes so we can collect the data and prove we are doing the work. This helps to fill the gap between the time we start and the time we can deliver, because sometimes the work won't be delivered for months at a time. Unfortunately, in many organizations, there is a lack of trust between IT and the business. This often stems from a history of perceived slowness or not delivering what IT said they would deliver. IT spends a boatload of time in traditional waterfall methods proving that they are doing the work rather than doing the work.

My perspective on process has changed a lot over the years. Fifteen years ago, you would often hear me say, "Follow the process because the process makes you safe" but safe shouldn't be your goal - delivering work should be your goal. Obviously, if your leader or organization requires these process steps to be completed so they can see you are working, there's a breakdown in trust. As an individual contributor, you can't fix that for the organization. But if you are leading a data team, perhaps now is the time to think about the transition to an agile framework.

This chapter will not teach you how to "Do Agile" or "Be Agile," for that you will have to go elsewhere (see the reading list in the appendix). What it will do is introduce some agile concepts you can consider in your data governance efforts.

The issues with data governance are layered. First, it's a definitional problem. We throw everything at data governance from definitions and usage to protection and security. We hang on to parochial methods of data governance with documentation, such as policies and procedures. We keep committees at the top, bury the people that do the work in a department and scatter decision-making rights between the people that know (i.e. stewards) and the people that have leadership responsibility (i.e. the executives). Most people realize that these methods don't often work; because it's a framework that we are familiar with, though, we stick to it. However, the way you're comfortable with isn't always the best way.

Another significant (and perhaps the most impactful) issue with data governance in a modern data platform is the volatility of the data itself. The data is coming into your systems at a high rate of speed and is always changing. So, if the purpose of governance is to create a lock and dam system to control the uncontrollable, how do you do that when volatility is all over the place? In other words, one day you're in the middle of a drought and the next day it's a 100-year-flood.

It is high time that we use modern methods to address our modern problem. Adopting agile methods, and leveraging DataOps and DevOps frameworks, we can begin to shore up the challenges we face in our broken governance programs. DataOps (see above) capabilities are gaining steam for good reason, and I believe this framework is a good starting point for a modern approach to data governance.

DataOps is an amalgamation of agile, lean and DevOps specifically geared to support data and analytics efforts. In the "DataOps" manifesto it shares these values:

- Individuals and interactions over processes and tools
- Working analytics over comprehensive documentation
- Customer collaboration over contract negotiation
- Experimentation, iteration, and feedback over extensive upfront design
- Cross-functional ownership of operations over siloed responsibilities[1]

I'll refer to this new method as Data Governance Operations (DGOps); it values usage of the data over the protection of an asset. It values the ability of teams to self form to address issues in the data, it sees all people across the organization as stewards of the data at different times for different purposes. It encourages questions of the data and it's quality because that only increases the knowledge and value of the data itself. In chapter seven we will delve a little deeper into the DGOps concept.

---

[1] https://bit.ly/2k0O3yc.

Stuff to stop doing

If we've learned anything over the last decade or two working in data governance it's that semantics, or what we call things, is important. Before I dive deeper into the "how" of using agile concepts for data governance, I want to update the language that is often used in governance.

It's time to get rid of the word "control." It implies something that's not achievable in a modern data platform. In addition, rather than creating a "standard" definition for our metrics, we should strive to create a "working" definition (WD), which allows for changes to occur, because changes will inevitably occur. Our goal should be to increase resiliency and the ability to respond to supposed anomalies occurring in the data. If we frame our governance efforts around creating standards, then we are starting off on the wrong foot.

As I was thinking through this work, I reached out to agile coach Kevin Burns. Kevin is a prolific lean and agile product development coach in the Twin Cities. He has a passion for helping teams turn their product ideas into implementations. As he and I discussed these concepts in the context of data governance, Kevin offered this: "Rather than a command and control frame, strive instead for adaptability and resiliency using visibility, pattern recognition, problem identification, decision criteria, problem-solving methods and deployment (release) using agile methods."

The best thing we can do is aim for improvement, and that's what agile methods bring to bear.

Stuff to start doing

I am still a proponent of defining your key organizational metrics. You should do that proactively. Just don't get wrapped around the axle and don't have too many metrics to start with. Create a list of key metrics the organization considers valuable and supports the decisions the organization needs to make. The executives should identify this list. The goal for the key metrics is to create a WD people can agree on. The intent is not to force everyone to use this one definition, but rather reach a level of agreement that encourages different parts of your organization to use these WDs when talking with each other. It addresses the part of governance that often gets touted, but rarely works well; making sure your executives are all looking at the same well-defined information.

There are some things in data governance that are still important and do work well. One of the key tenets to good DG is visibility and communication. Find like-minded people throughout your organization that either currently uses or want to use the metrics that are on your shortlist. I call this your analytic community. Every organization has them; few use them wisely.

Pull together this team of cross-functional analysts to discuss how different groups use these pre-defined organizational metrics – but beware of *analysis paralysis*. It is really easy to analyze and re-analyze and find yourself down a rabbit hole or on another topic altogether. Analysts, in particular, want to make sure that they have considered and vetted every conceivable use of the metric and every nuance of the data. Recently, I was talking with a former CIO of a hospital who said it took them eighteen months to uniquely define and measure "weight of a patient". I asked her, "What were people using while the governance team was working on the definition?" They continued to use the "old" definitions, or something that was probably *good enough*.

It's very likely that this team of cross-functional analysts will get together and then it will spiral. That's why it's critical that you identify your definition of done, success criteria, and/or good-enough-for-now criteria before you start. These are long-standing concepts in agile methods and ones that will bring the most value to our new approach to DG. We need to recognize that we're in a continuous state of learning, adapting, adjusting, and evolving. This helps us avoid analysis paralysis and helps get you to a minimally valuable product (MVP). In our new DGOps language, that's our "good enough" WD. This WD has to be based on our current understanding. If we agree that there is no inherent value in the process and that, in all likelihood while we're off analyzing data to get the definition perfect, the end-users are using good enough definitions anyway, the decision to adopt these agile principles should be obvious.

Another way to ensure that the team won't go off the rails, especially as you start this new way of thinking, is to consider a time limit or time-box for the discussion. If you follow the standard agile approach, you will have "sprints" or short cycles of work effort. Within a sprint, identify a limit of time in which you are willing to analyze the metric. You can use a few time-boxes first to do the data profiling and then test a couple of definitions, but then you should be prepared to propose a WD. Drive the discussion using the questions you need to be answered to make decisions to move forward (i.e. what business areas need to use the metric for decision-making). Then there should be some analysis related to questions you're unable to answer from the discussion (a little data mining to see if there are obvious things you've missed). This will likely involve data profiling work that will be done by the Quality Control (QC) team members. The importance of the analysis work is two-fold; first, to make sure the data supports how it will be used (sad to say that sometimes it doesn't!), and second, an understanding of how to implement changes once the team is ready to release the working definition.

Your QC team should create a data quality dashboard of (at a minimum) the key metrics so that at any given time, anyone can see how the data quality lines up. That level of visibility drives trust.

The steps

1. Work with your executive sponsor(s) to identify a finite list of metrics the organization will use (ideally, less than fifteen)
2. A group of executives should rank order those metrics
3. Find your analytic community
4. Bring together a cross-functional team of analysts and data quality resources to discuss the metric of choice
5. Use business terms to define the metric
6. Use math terms to define the algorithm that supports the metric
7. Run standard data profiling methods on all the data that make up the metric
8. Review the data with the cross-functional team for errors, nuances, and insights
9. Edit or modify either the definition or the algorithm based on what you learned with the data (important step!)
10. Publish your working definition
11. Gather feedback, edit and repeat

These steps can be included in your product backlog, a list of all the work that you are undertaking to achieve a product. In this case the product is a set of pre-defined working definitions for the organizational metrics commonly used for decision-making.

Working definitions and the idea of "good enough" is actually difficult to operationalize. Recently, in a conversation with a client, they asked "what about the changes? If we focus on good enough and we realize that it wasn't, how do we make the change?" It's a good question, but even the question hints at a waterfall mindset. The question assumes there's no value in the process. If we revisit the earlier example about the hospital defining weight in eighteen months and apply the DGOps method to it, the scenario might go something like this:

The weight of a patient in a pediatric hospital is a significant issue. It's often difficult to track reliably and critical for patient safety. Most pediatric hospitals have many ways of defining weight, both categorically (i.e. grams versus pounds) and process (babies are weighed laying down, older children on a traditional scale). Comparisons are difficult and for all of these reasons, it's important to govern and have consistency. Now that we've established weight as a key metric, within our DGOps method what's next? We review all the data typically associated with weight and where it is sourced from and where it goes to, including all the steps in between. During this time, we communicate frequently to as many stakeholders as possible (i.e.

our self-creating teams). If we meet, it's to review the data - not theories about the data (i.e. everyone's definitions). During this phase we learn from one another about the metric (weight in this case) but are likely still using the "old" way of defining it until we can find a better way.

The difference between the DGOps way and the previous method is that we encourage people to continue to use the data. We review the data as it exists in our systems and we take the time to learn about the data and how people use it AS-IS. Everyone is a steward in DGOps because at one point or another, everyone is using the data for different reasons. This creates an opportunity for process changes where they are most impactful (for instance, if one unit develops a better way to take a measurement, other units could adopt it). It also alleviates the pressure on everyone to agree to one standard definition for all cases, because there is no value in that.

After all versions of the data has been vetted, and broken processes are fixed, the team has learned and shared a lot about the data, all while using it. Then and only then can we all agree on a definition that the organization can use to compare. That definition would pass all of our tests (litmus and coded) and doesn't violate how the data is generated (defining and using data as it exists). Just as in any agile or Ops method, testing and visibility are the keys to acceptance of the data.

You break it we fix it

Because we will only be creating a WD for the limited set of metrics, you will find that there will be situations in which your users will discover data issues. It's important to know that this can be a good thing! That means they are using the data and it gives you an opportunity to dig into any data issue and determine what the problem really is.

For break/fix issues you will also want to take advantage of your backlog. Not all issues are created the same, nor are they of equal importance and it will not be feasible to track down everything. You will need to create a mechanism for your organization's response and ability to prioritize these things. This typically entails a quick review to determine the impact and severity of the issue.

For example, if one of your WDs is found to have an issue, it will likely carry more priority than an obscure metric issue that only impacts one person in one department. Try hard to avoid the fireman phenomenon (running from fire to fire putting them out as fast as you can) when you're structuring your break/fix capability. Rely heavily on your product owner to help triage the urgency and importance of requests.

DataOps

A few years ago, on my agile journey, I turned to Google – like most people do these days. I was looking for information regarding the use of agile concepts or examples of using agile methods for data programs. I came across the DataOps Manifesto (www.dataopsmanifesto.org). I remember reading it and filing it away in the back of my head. Then as I started research for this book, I re-visited the Manifesto and had the opportunity to talk with one of the co-writers, Christopher Bergh, CEO and Head Chef of DataKitchen. I talked with a lot of people about this book, but the conversation with Chris felt like it lasted ten minutes, but I took the full hour. We were in what I like to call "violent agreement" about the value of DataOps for data programs.

In the manifesto there are eighteen principles; you should read them all. I cherry-picked a few because this isn't a chapter on the manifesto, it's a chapter on how to take the concepts and use it for a process update in governance.

The gist of the manifesto for our purposes is this: analytics is a team sport. Focus on getting the data or results of the analysis into the hands of users, something data governance should address as well. Visibility to the process (including testing and code) is integral to success, because it helps build trust. As I outlined in the first paragraph, most organizations actually place value on the process itself. They turn to the steps in the process and check them off like they've accomplished something. They use that to pretend they're providing visibility into the work they do. They won't show you the work, but they will show you that they spent ten hours on step fifteen in the project plan. The transition to agile and DGOps requires a degree of visibility and transparency that makes the people who have been using the old methods for a long time very uncomfortable. Particularly in analytics, we have come to believe that the quality of the data is OUR job, and ours alone.

Many of us don't believe that other people in the organization have the capability to understand what we are doing or how we are doing it. But that's beside the point. Understanding isn't always the goal. If you can't provide transparency to the process, anything you say about a delay becomes a trust issue. As Chris said in our conversations "Hope and trust are important feelings to have, but they don't belong in analytics." Our users shouldn't "hope" for great work and we shouldn't force them to "trust" us without the willingness to back that up. There is no question that the transition to DGOps and agile methods will be disruptive to your organization and to your staff. You've already done it the other way and it hasn't worked. What's wrong with trying it a new way? Even if DGOps doesn't work for your organization, you will still probably learn a lot. Keep making improvements, because that's all any of us can ask for continuous improvement.

It might be worth your time to consider an even bolder step, one that requires you to blend together the changes in the people and roles, with the changes in the process. Most agile experts will tell you that change in the roles is as important as changes in the process. Self-creating teams and product owners are the things that catapult most agile efforts to the next level of velocity. I've seen this firsthand; through a humbling experience I had as I managed my first agile team.

One of the things I really like about agile, at least how we were doing it in this particular project was the exposure to the data. I had data points showing how much time someone thought something was going to take against how long it actually took. Every two weeks I would happily sit down with my Excel sheet and calculate out the accuracy of individuals and make (what I thought was) helpful adjustments to the work to ensure that we improved our accuracy of estimates. My thinking was the closer our accuracy, the better the projections of the model. The better the projections, the easier time I had sharing it with executives. After a while I noticed our completion or close rate start to diminish at a much higher rate than I could rationally explain. Our due date kept pushing out and I was getting nervous. I'd call a meeting together and we would fiddle with the model to see what we were missing. The team would sit there quietly and listen to me pontificate on the importance of velocity. A few brave souls would raise their hand and tell me why something took longer, and I always had a (useless) management-like response.

After a while, I was in full panic mode, so I called in David (the big guns). By this point David had been diagnosed with cancer and was actively in treatment. I was only hoping for a bit of an email exchange, but he offered to come in. There's a lot I can say about that day: the energy in the room, the discussions we had, and the fact that David was tired and weak, but as insightful as ever. But what I learned that day changed everything for me. I learned that I was the problem. I was so busy being helpful I was messing people up. The problem with our velocity wasn't the team or their ability to accurately determine the work effort... it was me! I was in their hair all the time mucking up their flow. Talk about an exercise in humility. I had always prided myself on being the person that helped my team members become the best versions of themselves. On that day, though, I realized that I had been forcing them to be the best version of what *I thought* they *should* be, slowing down the project in the process.

I took a deep breath and I stepped back. I worked with good, smart people, and I needed to let them do good, smart work. Immediately, they began to self-organize, create the backlog, and work through their own issues. I was always there when they got stuck, and I still prioritized the backlog, but it was different. They felt it and I felt it. And you know what happened? Our velocity tripled.

Prioritization and product owners

Now here's the thing about having lots of analysts doing lots of things for lots of different people in your organization: it produces a natural conflict for prioritization. Every organization has limitations to what they can do; whether that's with the number of people they can hire or with the amount of money they can invest in a data asset. Eventually, you will find yourself in a situation where analysts (or ambassadors) have competing projects. They might all have great endpoints, but you cannot get them done at the same time.

Typically, this is the point where I would recommend that you create a committee of people that can review all the requests and prioritize them based on the value they provide and/or the effort they take. I still make that recommendation to lots of organizations but if you are ready to take on a truly agile way of thinking about delivery incremental deliverables are key. The idea of holding onto things until a committee can get together and review them flies in the face of many of the key attributes of agile and DataOps Manifesto and our newly minted DGOps. What's a product owner to do?

First, make sure you really have a conflict. Sometimes things seem difficult, labor-intensive or contradictory on the surface, but turn out to be none of those things upon digging deeper. Instead, it's the people involved artificially introducing barriers, for different reasons. Here's one example: you have a small request from the business that's being pushed out 3 -4 sprints from now. The business doesn't understand why it takes that long, and frankly neither do you. You realize the issue isn't the work itself, it's that there's only one analyst with the skill set to complete it – and they are fully utilized. You have a bottleneck issue, not a complex problem requiring a team to solution and debate. Do what you need to do to solve the problem in the short term and make a note that you have some cross-training to do in the future.

Agile is designed for the work to be able to shift between resources as needed, but sometimes in data, particularly in smaller organizations, you don't have the luxury of that level of redundancy. Even if you've been savvy in hiring and know very well that someone has those skills, there is a cost to context shifting (see box below) that you need to be aware of. The main thing you need to consider is this: you value progress over committee reviews and delays.

Prioritize the work that you think has value and can be done quickly, move work around to different resources when you can and help your stakeholders understand the challenges you are facing. Changes can be made both in deliverables and prioritizations when you all agree on a minimally viable product. That's harder to do when your organization or team is all geared toward traditional waterfall methods.

> "When you focus on one particular type of task, challenge, or information set, then switch to something completely different, you're shifting contexts. Sometimes, the transitions are huge and jarring. Other times, you don't even notice them."[2]

Love Your errors

Probably the biggest change I'm proposing to traditional governance is the idea of radically democratizing access to data. You have to get data out there, let people use it, find things "wrong" with it, and even ask terrible questions. You must learn to love the errors inherent in the data and stop trying to prevent them after the fact. I know that sounds categorically insane for a data professional to claim, but it's true. Governance has become too much about protection from people using the data and not enough about promotion. The only way that we can get the full capability from the data assets we are so worried about protecting is to let them go a little and be there to pick up the pieces when terrible stuff happens. And it will happen. Adjusting your mindset toward ambassadorship and first responders allows you to protect what you can and prepare for the rest/worst. Using the DGOps model helps take incremental steps to improve the data,

---

[2]https://bit.ly/2zuzgzV.

but it also helps us frame the usage of data into a functioning data governance capability.

Love the errors you find in the data. Don't hide them, this only makes your job more difficult and lets the people or process responsible for the error off the hook. As so eloquently described in the DataOps Cookbook, analytics is a team sport and for too long we have let our executives and users get away with nominal engagement. We brushed their lack of participation off by saying it was too difficult or that it was "our job," but data is nothing without context. The only way to provide context is through business knowledge. Active participation in a self-created team to deliver incremental value helps everyone understand their role in stellar data governance.

The shift to an agile or DGOps mindset is not insignificant. In the appendix of this book, you will find a curated list of recommended reading, based on my many great conversations with others on this subject. Take the time to read some of those other books; talk to other people that have made the shift, and help your organization prepare for some of the changes, or at least acknowledge that there could be huge value in doing so. Then, hire a coach to help you through the transition. Don't worry about software or tools right away. Take the time to get the process stuff figured out; tools should come *after* you understand the value you need from them. Give yourself time as the change happens. Some of the biggest lessons I learned during my agile transition had to do with how I led the team. Leading and supporting your staff through this transition looks a lot like parenting. You give them the foundation they need to make good decisions, and you're there to dust them off when they stumble and encourage them to keep going.

Wrapping it up

There is no end to data governance. It will run long past your tenure. Building a resilient program requires resilient processes. Instead of proving you're doing the work you're just doing the work. The one thing I want you to remember from this chapter is to keep making incremental progress. Data governance, perhaps more than any other data function, is an unrelenting foe. The only way to tame it is to be vigilant, don't expect a big bang, just keep moving forward and focusing on building minimally valuable products, showing value and improving every day.

CHAPTER 3

Technology

I am down to the wire. This book is due in just a few weeks and as I was sending content out to be edited, I decided to delete chapter four completely. I needed to start over with a completely blank page. Why? Because the first iteration of this chapter was terrible. I danced around subjects, made thinly veiled recommendations, and yammered on a lot about software. If I could barely read it, how could I expect anyone else to?

I am not a technologist; I'm actually an analyst by training. Moreover, I'm a woman in a male-dominated industry (which *shouldn't* matter, but it does). I censor myself when it comes to technology to avoid the inevitable know-it-all bully. I'm talking about the person who will rate this whole book as a failure, because I didn't go deep into some arbitrary technology, or explain in nauseating detail the danger of Cartesian joins.

A few years ago, my then-boss told me not to let anyone bully me, because I knew way more than I let on. That's true, after twenty years of working in and around data warehouses I can stand toe-to-toe in some pretty technical conversations. I recognize when people are purposefully trying to obfuscate the issue by using technical terms. My hesitation was reflected in the chapter. So when my first editor said, "something is weird about chapter four, I just can't put my finger on it," I knew I had to make some big changes.

Data Governance is not about technology

While this chapter is dedicated to the idea that technology can solve problems associated with data governance, there's one thing I have to get out of the way first. Fixing data governance is not really about technology. No technology in the world can save your data governance program from itself. I don't care if the technology is an AI bot that will not sleep until it tracks down every errant piece of data. Technology can't solve broken processes, lack of people, lack of knowledge of the people, or poorly defined functions. Technology is only as good as the implementer, the user, and the purpose. If you have no clear purpose, misaligned users, or implementers that say yes (or no) to every customization, then all you have is another mess on your hands.

What technology can do is solve well-defined problems. But you must know exactly what those problems are and *why* they are actually problems. In this chapter we will look at the options we have today with technology and data governance. The choices are vast and compelling. There are exciting advancements in capabilities that include machine learning (ML) and artificial intelligence (AI). There are really exciting tools that finally give our end-users a view into disparate data sets and their quality. We will explore these options and set a clear path to what problems they can tangibly solve in your journey to modern data governance.

There is too much data for us not to use software to improve it. Even some of the most advanced tools we have don't do a great job at improving data quality, because they're waiting for a human to tell them what to do. The trouble is, humans are often wrong or imply their version of reality on top of the data, whether they realize it or not. The best we can do is to let the data tell us what it should be, and then we review it to determine if that fits our expectations. If expectations are misaligned, the job is to review our expectations and processes for how the data got there. At the end of the day, it is really that simple. The data is neither good nor bad, it's just data.

A refresher

Data governance has typically been about providing context associated with the data. Simply, one of the main jobs of data governance was to create a standard definition of data. Of course, there were other things like protection of the data and quality of the data, but context was really the core of data governance. For a long time, we tried to create one definition of something, like patient. But as time went on something curious happened. Data professionals realized that it's not possible to define everything in your data warehouse. Even if you could, someone would always disagree with you. Historically, context drove the definition, the definition drove the quality, and quality was the thing you could "implement" into the data warehouse - that process broke down so often though. Data was too dirty and data quality processes could barely keep up. To compensate, data engineers introduced large sets of transformation code to bend the data to match definitions, but the trouble is, that's not scalable. Projects are under pressure to get the work done quickly and on time. Often, as a result, QA and UAT are reduced to only a few days. We forsake the time needed to do the work thoroughly.

The summer after I graduated high school I worked in a plastics factory. I've had just about every job you can imagine, but let me tell you: you have not lived until you've spent a hot summer in an even hotter factory.

What I learned from my time there was short but important:

1. It was hard work and I didn't like it, so I better do well at college
2. A pallet of plastic pellets makes a lot of very different kind of stuff

Analogies abound in data work. But a factory is pretty relevant when it comes to data governance. You take raw materials and make them into something less raw. If you were a factory owner and you had a pallet of white plastic pellets, would you look at that and say, "We will only make paper towel holders from this raw material?" No, you would look at that giant box of white pellets as raw material that could be transformed into anything. We need to let the data help us see what it could be, not just from a definitional perspective, but also from a quality perspective. With new technology capabilities, it is feasible to look at more of the data than ever before. See what fits into your definition and what doesn't. Do gut checks against it with your business end-users. Fix the data entry processes that create terrible data or adjust the definitions if they don't reflect the reality. It's still okay, and in many cases necessary, to know how your organization needs to define key metrics. But now the technology allows us to make that even easier by laying bare the data issues earlier than ever. Here's another analogy for you: we should stop trying to put the water back into the river after a flood and look to see what caused the flood in the first place.

How to train your data

The premise is simple. Can you use AI, or more specifically ML methods and tools, to improve the quality of your data for your enterprise? I asked some smart people this question, people actually working in AI/ML tech, to weigh in.

The first time I heard the term "AI washing" was when I interviewed Neil Raden for the chapter. Simply, AI washing is when a company claims they are using advanced tech like AI in their products, but they're really not. Neil talked about an article that was based on assessments of European start-ups, although I doubt this issue is limited to that region. The article claimed that forty percent of the companies surveyed had no AI capabilities, despite claiming they did. Just a few months ago I had the opportunity to review a large software company's analytics package that claimed to leverage "AI capabilities" to speed the scale of data ingestion. I was told the coding would get faster and better as more data was ingested, which would (in theory) reduce costs as the scope increased. In reality, we found the reverse to be as we tried to increase the scope during the initial contract phase. So, I did a little research, tracked down someone who used to work at this company, and they confirmed that it was really people scaling the system, not AI capabilities.

With so much misinformation out there what is a leader supposed to do? I have found this to be true in the data industry quite often over the past two decades. It's pretty easy to write a great article or throw a glossy brochure together and hope for the best. It's a common sales practice and oddly enough the more complicated the tech gets, the easier it is for software companies to pull the proverbial wool over our eyes.

Let's wade through the muck of machine learning and artificial intelligence to determine if there is a value to data quality. Together we will learn the definitions, the reality of the industry and a method to evaluate AI-driven tech.

Right brain left brain

I have come to think about it like this. If artificial intelligence is the thing that gets all the attention, takes what we know and turns it into decisions, actions, art, or music, it's like our right brain. The machine learning takes the data and categorizes it for us, indexes it into constructs that are easy for us to navigate. Think about when you learn something new: you scan first, then categorize, and finally, you develop a new way of thinking. Machine learning is our left brain, scanning and categorizing the mammoth amount of information that is available today.

In order to break down the feasibility of using ML to improve our enterprise data quality I did two things: determined what we meant by data quality and then reviewed the science and statistics behind the machine learning algorithms.

In order to help our ML algorithms train the data to improve, I first needed to know what good data quality looks like. To understand this, I turned to Steve Johnson, professor at the University of Minnesota. Steve is on a personal mission to use data to solve some of the world's biggest problems. Not long after setting this goal, however, he realized that he wouldn't get far until the data improved. As such, he took a slight detour from his original mission to clearly define and operationalize what we meant by "Good Data Quality" (GDQ). Steve and a group of other researchers have been at it for over two years now. They have agreed on a standard subset of elements that make up good data quality. [3]

1. Conformance: Do Data Values Adhere to Specified Standards and Formats
    a) Value Conformance
    b) Relational Conformance
    c) Computational Conformance
2. Completeness: Are Data Values Present
3. Plausibility: Are Data Values Believable
    a) Uniqueness Plausibility
    b) Atemporal Plausibility
    c) Temporal Plausibility

---

[3] Harmonized Data Quality Terminology and Framework, (2016) Kahn et al, eGEMS.

Each of these categories can be broken down into definitions, examples, and subcategories. While this system was initially created for healthcare use, simple changes to definitions and examples make it clear that there is value outside of healthcare. To be sure, this framework is a broad swipe at the details associated with data quality. It is one that helps us start at the beginning; first, does the data exist, next, is it structured similarly (i.e. format) and finally, do we believe it. One would argue that these are at the heart of what it means to have GDQ.

These align well with the standard definitions of data quality for data warehouses that we review in chapter six:

- Completeness
- Uniqueness
- Timeliness
- Validity
- Accuracy
- Consistency

ML framework

Watch any video on ML or talk to anyone in the field and they will start by explaining how ML works. To understand these concepts, you may have to brush off some of your basic stats books from back in the day (I hope you didn't sell them at a garage sale). There are three ways that ML algorithms work:

1. Supervised Learning
2. Unsupervised Learning
3. Reinforcement Learning

Simply stated, supervised learning is using labeled data sets to show the algorithm what's what. Unsupervised learning uses unlabeled data. The deliverable is a chart (like a scatter plot) that attempts to display relationships with the data, back to good old-fashioned linear regression. The final one is reinforcement learning, and that is teaching the system through correction.

AI/ML in data governance

Now that we know how to define GDQ and we understand the basic framework of ML, I think it's a short step to the idea that ML can help improve data quality at an enterprise level. But we can quickly run into trouble without a solid and responsive data governance foundation, because humans need to provide enough context to support supervised learning, as well as effective guidance for unsupervised and reinforcement learning, or the ML application will just become another "fun" technology project.

Some data quality organizations understand this intuitively and have built products that make data quality part of everyone's job. Trifacta is a company that has attempted to do just that. Through simplistic yet elegant applications of ML and an intuitive user interface, the software helps everyone in the organization see the data and respond to it. Trifacta uses the terms "Active" and "Passive" wherein the active allows users to profile and do "smart cleaning," addressing issues common in the GDQ framework, such as missing data and inconsistent formats of the data. The passive provides the ability to monitor data with rules applied to ensure consistency. One could argue that if all analysts in your organization had this capability at their fingertips, the transparency could drive organizational shifts in the responsibility of data quality. That's a critical step in changing the way that data quality is worked on.

Data catalogs

Every year in late July or early August, something special would come in the mail. It was the Sears catalog. I grew up in a remote area, with few clothing stores around, so buying new school clothes was either a matter of a day trip to the "big city" or simply day-dreaming my way through the Sears catalog. The catalog was huge, probably three inches thick and heavy. It's like printing out your last three months of search history on Amazon.

As a young kid, I didn't really consider the effort it took to put that catalog together. I didn't consider that each item in that catalog likely came from a different source and that while a number of them looked the same, they were quite different. Polo shirts were big back then and you could get one in just about any color. I got mine in light blue, to match my striped pants, then I'd throw my pink sweater around my shoulders with the arms loosely crossing in front, but I digress. The point is, creating a catalog of similar items allowed me (my mother actually) the ease of picking from similar but distinct items based on our requirements. My neighbor chose a different polo based on her requirements. I think you get the idea. Fast-forward to today where we have data catalogs that allow for easy access to similar but distinct data. These data catalogs show you where the data comes from, and allow you, based on your requirements, to pick your own data. For example, if I'm working in finance, the data I'm interested in has to come from the accounts payable software I interact with, not the other downstream systems that use that data. I'm going to look for the data or metric that comes from the system I'm used to using. The same goes for just about every other operational function you can imagine.

This seems a bit contrary to the historical view of data governance where we integrate everything and define certain metrics that the whole organization must use - but it's not the antithesis it's an evolution. Knowing it's not possible for us to scale to every data point in every source system we have to allow for the need of our end-users to access the data that's most relevant to their work. Data catalogs allow for a seamless, visually appealing way of doing that. They provide the lineage of the data (i.e. technical metadata) and many of them can be modified, based on governance standards, to show different weights for certain data. For example, if you have a customer identifier and the source of that identifier is Salesforce. As that customer ID is used in every conceivable system in your environment, you can place a weight on the Salesforce version of that ID, so the user knows which ID started all the downstream processes. That's a simple example, but an important method to provide more context to the capabilities of data catalogs in terms of data governance.

Data catalogs are a tool for your users to access the data that's "good enough" for their purposes until they need more in-depth capabilities. The value of these products can't be understated in the era of modern data governance. If helping people use the data is now at least half of our goal of governance, providing the tools so people can see all the choices and pick from them is a great start. It may be all some of your users will ever need. It also helps with something else, something not intended, but clearly a consequence. If your users see all of the data that is similar but not identical, it may help them understand the difficult undertaking of integrating the data together. Each of these systems uses machine learning and artificial intelligence in varying degrees.

Where to start

Tracking your disparate data to determine its quality and usability is a pretty exciting thing for a data geek. I haven't been this excited about a software solution in a while. Data catalogs really do offer a lot of value to your data governance effort, but we need to make sure we are solving the right problem.

Oddly enough, as I was in the midst of this research, I met the indelible Jen Underwood. I met Jen at a conference and we shared an instant connection. Then, happily, I found an article she wrote about the requirements for a data catalog purchase.

Jen's Requirements:

1. Automated, intelligent population of the catalog
2. Crowd-sourced curation of tags with machine learning feedback
3. Crowd-sourced ratings and reviews
4. Ability to ensure tagging and metadata freshness
5. Enterprise scalability
6. Open API's for integration with a wide variety of tools
7. Search
8. Data catalog as a platform
9. Data lineage
10. Data protection

You can read Jen's entire blog about her requirements here: https://bit.ly/2jX4njn.

I would add to Jen's list a few other considerations:

1. Platform Agnostic
2. Integrated Data Prep
3. Security
4. The overall product roadmap
5. Natural language search

There are a lot of data catalog tools available in the market. If we've seen anything in the data industry, it's that we like to consolidate across platforms. I would watch for a data catalog that is platform-agnostic, so it can catalog data from anywhere, not just its own native databases.

Some catalogs integrate data prep, and that is a very compelling feature for over-worked data engineers. I would also add that security should be on the list. For what may be the first time, your company will be able to see most, if not all, of your data. If you don't already have a solid security protocol on the databases themselves or across the platforms, you may want to see what access management options are available in the data catalog itself.

As with any software acquisition know where the vendor sits in terms of financial viability and long-term product roadmap.

Does it look like they are positioning to be acquired? Do you care?

One important variable that we haven't addressed yet is the data at the source. These tools and methods can address the data once it's out of the source system, but the "bad" processes that created the "bad" data will persist until addressed. This is where transparency may be a more important consideration than the GDQ work itself. Data catalogs have filled this gap.

For many years we had virtually no technology tools that would help provide a seamless layer over all of the potential data sources. Utilizing ML functions, data catalogs have the ability to go trolling your data sources and bring to bear a visual representation of data lineage. It's a compelling option.

Whether you follow the new modern data platform rules or prefer a federated approach to data, it can nicely tie up what could otherwise be a messy platform, at least from an end-user perspective. But be wary, during my interviews and conversations with people, a number of analytic leaders recognized the potential, but also the pitfall. One leader said to me, "If I did this the way it's recommended, they'd be trolling databases all the time, slowing stuff down, with very little value."

It's just a tool

Regardless of the tech, however bright and shiny it is or what the vendor promises you, please keep an eye on the value ball. My husband has thousands of dollars' worth of fancy woodworking tools in the garage. They're the best tools for their function, but they collect dust just like the $10 hammer I bought at Target over twenty years ago. Tools are only as good at the person using it. The things that tools help build or support need the business case to balance the expense. I have one really nice table he built me - pretty sure it doesn't balance out with the money we invested in it. Don't tell him I told you that though!

If you know you have issues with data quality but are worried about the ROI of the work effort (as you should be), creating a baseline framework for what the data looks like (data profiling) and sharing that broadly (democratizing), may yield better results than aiming for something more abstract, at least in the beginning. I'm a big believer in KISS. Not the band (they are awesome!), the acronym Keep It Simple Stupid (sorry for the non-PC version). You should know what you are trying to fix or improve *before* you start throwing money at the problem. Implementing software can feel like progress until someone taps you on the shoulder and asks you the value you got from the investment you made. You will eventually have to find a technical method of improving data quality and I really do believe that ML and associated products are the way forward. But sometimes, it's better to start where it's really broken.

Data Quality Dashboard

If you consider your data as a value chain, the weakest link will be poor data quality. The challenge with data quality is multi-faceted. It's one of the reasons why every organization I have ever talked to has asked about how to improve data quality. It doesn't matter if the organization has been doing analytics for years or if they just started down the analytics journey. Data quality has become our Achilles heel. Now, data governance and data quality are not the same things, but as I said in an earlier chapter, there is no data governance without data quality and there is no data quality without data governance. They must exist together in a symbiotic relationship.

Part of the function of data governance is to identify the key metrics for the organization, define them, and ensure they have good data quality. It is not all that governance does, but an important part. Our executives should have a line of sight to a handful of metrics that they use to run the organization. There is some required discipline to get to less than fifteen metrics (extra points for ten). Once you get there, you should create a data quality dashboard that simply shows a summary page of how "good" that data is for the integrated metric. For clarity, a metric usually requires a numerator and a denominator. The dashboard shows the metric as a ratio, and a separate tab should absolutely include the numerator and denominator. For example, in healthcare, there is a ratio of per member per month, essentially a breakdown of the cost of a member (someone that is participating in a health plan). Our dashboard should show the PMPM for that month, perhaps a sparkline to show the history of that metric and in the second tab should also show the member counts per month along with the cost. You should be able to easily see the change the metric goes through over time. If it's a very stable metric, a run chart is a great visual. There are also color-based examples, making the metric turn shades of red/yellow/green if it starts to shift between expected ranges.

The expected ranges for those ten to fifteen metrics should be well known. This type of data quality dashboard is at the end of your data factory, if you will. The data catalog monitors the data quality of the raw materials; this will show your end-users the quality of the end result of your effort. Obviously, if the data catalog shows the raw data going south, there will be a corresponding reflection of that in the data quality dashboard. This dashboard is meant for the average user or even an executive, not an analyst. It helps provide transparency and acknowledgment that you understand how important data quality is to the organization. It's like a stamp of quality or freshness.

The primary idea here is that there are no surprises with the data associated with the key metrics that run your organization; get that right! You can't have this level of knowledge on every piece of data, and not every piece of data warrants the time and cost associated with this level of work. This takes discipline, and the understanding that not all data is created equal.

Wrapping it up

First, technology is just a tool. It can't fix bad processes or people issues. Make sure that you know exactly what the tech will address for your organization and that there is a solid return on investment. Second, there are a lot of advantages to data catalogs. I still don't think it's the first thing you do, but for the first time, you have a line of sight to data in disparate systems. That's too compelling to ignore. Pick your requirements that align well with how your organization thinks about data governance and data quality. Start small with a POC or pilot project. Third, data quality is the result of solid governance processes. As I've said before in this book, you need to deal with the people, processes and the culture, along with the tech. But if you do that excellent data quality will be the result.

CHAPTER 4

Data Culture and Change Management

It's time to talk about the elephant in the room. There's a famous saying that goes something like "Culture eats strategy for breakfast." In other words: you can have the best plan in the world, but if you don't consider organizational culture, all bets are off. As I was interviewing people for this book, a leader of analytics said, "Sometimes it seems the culture overrides logic." It's a sad acknowledgment of the reality of the effort.

I've said it before, but it's worth repeating; these programs are like an ecosystem and culture is the air we breathe. You can pretend culture is not there, you can pretend it doesn't matter, you can hold your breath waiting for it to change, but you *will* face the consequences eventually.

There's no question in my mind, of all the things that can ruin a data governance initiative, the culture of an organization is your top contender - even with the best of intentions and methods. An unwillingness to embrace change, an obstacle-focused viewpoint and the hero mentality, absolutely all of it (and more) will suffocate you.

Disruption

We need to have an increase in usage of the data, because we agreed that usage is the whole point. But usage also terrifies a lot of data professionals and executives alike. We are disrupting these data governance efforts—which requires effective change management.

We are purposefully disrupting data governance, because traditional implementations no longer work for most organizations and the amount of data they have today. Disruption though does not mean ill-conceived or improperly followed through.

And it's not just about the data; it's also about the speed at which most organizations today must operate. Businesses no longer have months to consider a shift, when your competitors can do it in weeks or days. Disruptive changes are happening in business models every day. Our leaders are feeling an enormous amount of pressure to get decisions right and data can help them. The velocity in which organizations have to review, consider, and shift means that we have to stay fluid and dynamic in our approach. Rigidity in approach leads to critical failures. That's why airplane wings can flex, and palm trees can withstand hurricane-force winds. Our governance structures must reflect the way we do business today; provide enough integrity to bend, but not break.

What is culture and why does it matter?

During the writing of this book, I sat in a roundtable discussion on the topic of "Making a change that sticks." The first question the moderator asked of the panel was "What is culture," because of course, you have to define the thing that you are changing before you can change it. Each panelist gave answers that felt directionally accurate, identifying the intangible aspect of the question, sharing that it's about the behaviors and values.

> **"Organizational culture** is a system of shared assumptions, values, and beliefs, which governs how people behave in organizations. These shared values have a strong influence on the people in the organization and dictate how they dress, act, and perform their jobs. Every organization develops and maintains a unique culture, which provides guidelines and boundaries for the behavior of the members of the organization."[4]

Culture is important because it quite literally defines and guides the organization and its employees on what is appropriate, and what's not. It is the framework in which all other things are measured. In many ways, it is intangible, or difficult to articulate to someone outside the organization. One of my favorite questions to ask when I'm interviewing with an organization is how they describe the culture. I'm looking for two things, of

---

[4] https://bit.ly/2KUq4Kr.

equal importance to me: the ability to answer the question (regardless of whether I like the answer), and the answer itself.

If the person I'm interviewing with is able to quickly and confidently answer this question, it likely means they keenly understand how essential and relevant culture is. It means they have thought about it enough to put words to it. You would be surprised how often I get answers like "well, I guess I'm not sure how I would describe it" or "that's really hard to do." More often than not, the people who have the hardest time answering the question about culture are the technology leaders. Think about that, the department that is responsible for introducing more disruptive change than any other cannot clearly articulate the culture. The thing you can't articulate will be the thing that gets you in the end.

The other important thing to me is *how* they answer the question. I look for a couple of attributes in a company I work with. Their willingness and openness to change, partnership, people-first mentality (both employees and customers) along with a certain something, an "it" factor if you will. Yes, that is intangible, but it's intangible because it's different for everyone.

Here's a good example: recently a mid-sized consulting firm that was looking to break into the data industry contacted me. They wanted to know what a data practice might look like for them. I get these calls a lot; everyone wants to be in data. We're finally the cool kids! I arrive on a sunny Thursday morning, dressed in business casual attire. I'm greeted by an iPad, a receptionist, and a dog named Max. In the reception area there are trendy chairs positioned askew around a live wood coffee table and a Sputnik light fixture dangling from a vaulted ceiling. Glass walls, similar to the ones you see at the zoo, keep me from hearing the conversation happening in the conference room to my left.

After a few minutes, a tall gentleman with an easy smile greets me and we take a quick tour around their facility. They are really proud of it, or so he tells me. A few things I notice: dog beds tucked under stand-up desks, twinkly lights, umbrellas, Star Wars and other nerdy paraphernalia everywhere, and (most importantly to me) no walls. None. Everyone had tiny desks linked together. Their culture didn't whisper, it screamed. It was embedded in every corner of the building.

This is what I mean by "it" factor. For me, as a middle-aged woman, the essence of the environment was not welcoming, but that's my perspective. I'm willing to bet a thirty-something man would've had a vastly different take on it - by design. Your culture is the way you present to and attract the world around you. It lures in like-minded people and is either the fertile or desolate ground in which you are now sowing your seed of change.

Data culture

In my second book "Data-Driven Healthcare" I postulated that "Data-Driven means information must be consumable and contextual, to encourage action that will modify behavior over time." I think this definition has stood the test of time and applies to data governance as well. If you can't modify behavior from the data, then what are you doing with it? The work to move your organization from gut-driven decision-making to data-driven decisions requires a multi-faceted approach. It requires your organization to adopt a data culture.

McKinsey has seven principles for a healthy data culture. If I hadn't have found it after most of the content for this book was written I would have quoted it more liberally. In the article, they represent many of the things that are positioned in this book including the need to position people first, acknowledge the risk inherent in the work, the need to get the data out there and many other spot-on principles of creating a data culture. [5]

Data cultures that imbue these principles are actually pretty rare. When they do occur, they tend to get a lot of press, awards, articles, etc. But the vast majority of organizations I've worked

[5] Diaz, Alejandro, Rowshankish, Kayvaun, Saleh, Tamim. (2018, September) McKinsey Quarterly. Why Data Culture Matters. https://mck.co/2wPN72R.

with over the years may have had a few of these – I can't think of a single one that had them all. I share this with you because it's important to understand that, as a data leader in your organization, you're probably not as behind as you think. For as long as I've been a consultant, I've also been an employee leading these efforts and I know the pressure cooker you're in. The constant drumbeat of "we need more data" and "you're too slow" buffered only by the "the data is wrong" and "how hard can this be?" Even if you're a positive person it's hard not to be frustrated by all of the naysayers and boisterous champions for your dismissal.

We have left the "data culture" conversation on the back burner for far too long because we didn't think it mattered. These gossamer-like threads we weave into organizations can fray so quickly when one person leaves or a new executive decides that data is a commodity (worry when an executive tells you that). The work to create a data culture is a change management effort; one that requires thoughtful, thorough and consistent management.

This is personal

It is of utmost importance that you recognize how personal this is to your team. Work is personal and anyone who says it isn't is looking for the easy button. It's personal because it's how we spend our time, our most valuable, non-renewable resource. Don't get me wrong, we are an industrious species, we like to stay busy, but we do have options. There are many diverse reasons your team picked your organization, but the fact remains: when the rubber hits the road, it *is* personal to them, and any change will create a high degree of distress.

It should be personal for you too. Why are you the pioneer of this change? Dig deep and make sure that you're doing this is for the right reasons, not because you were told or because you like to blow stuff up and see where it lands (I am a little embarrassed to admit that I often fall into that latter camp). You need to be willing to acknowledge that the work is personal, and to take the time to map out the impact of the change and manage it. If you're not willing to do that then stop here. Seriously, put the book down and go on with your day. It won't work without that personal commitment.

If you are ready, then let's start with a quick exercise to get you thinking about your organization and its readiness for change. I want you to label the issues you're seeing in your culture. This is not a right or wrong exercise, just a personal perspective based on your experiences. You don't have to be an expert in all things change-related to know what your challenges will be; you just have to have some level of awareness. For example, a lot of places trying to deploy data assets have a "hero culture," where the analysts will do crazy things to answer questions as fast as possible. While that feels great for the heroes at the moment, it often leads to scenarios that are not scalable or maintainable – and your heroes desperately overworked in short order. Perhaps you've noted a hesitation to take on new changes, whether at an executive level or an individual contributor level. Wherever the source, unwillingness to change is an issue. Spend some time scanning the organization, identifying where you see issues and document them.

Years ago I started seeing the impact culture and their inability to manage change had on my clients. I adopted a questionnaire that was published in Fortune magazine, an article written by Thomas Stewart in 1994. He had identified seventeen key elements to determine an organization's readiness for change. I used that questionnaire in conjunction with an analytics maturity model to help me frame what was likely going to be my client's biggest issues as they transitioned from decisions by the gut to decisions by data. Without fail, organizations with big culture issues were the ones who struggled with gaining traction.

The experts weigh in

There is value to any framework because they provide a "you are here" starting point, but they don't tell you what to do next, or how to break apart the work into manageable steps. For that, we seek out people that do change management for a living.

There is an enormous number of resources out there on this topic, so I needed to cull through some of the noise. To help with that, I reached out to Dan Olson. Dan is a veteran change agent and purveyor of compelling insights. He quickly cut to the chase by positing that the point of any change is to increase utilization and adoption. Of course, in data terms that easily equates to systems, software or data assets themselves.

Since we know that change is really about the individuals in the organization, we need to start by first understanding their perspective. Dan said he often starts with an empathy map, a term I'd not heard of before.

After doing a quick Internet search, I found that empathy maps are an evolution of user personas, work-types found in web design decades ago. Today it's often used in agile methods as well, so it's an excellent starting point for us. Empathy maps[6] briefly identify what a user or stakeholder in our change effort could be thinking, feeling, doing, or saying. In other words, we are going to put ourselves in their shoes for a bit. Here is an Empathy Map:

---

[6] https://adobe.ly/2Umc4Qe.

Say: Ideally you would use actual quotes from people that fall into this theme.	Think: What are they thinking about the upcoming change?
Do: What do you observe in their behavior?	Feel: What worries might the individual have about the change?

Obviously, it is unrealistic to do an empathy map for every person in your organization (I suppose if you have a company of thirty people you might try), so first take that list of issues you identified early on and create themes. Next, use those themes to create empathy maps. For example, let's make an empathy map for the individuals with "Hero Mentality":

Say: "I provide excellent customer service to people that ask for the data. I don't need you to improve stuff because I am already doing a great job, just ask them!"	Think: It's unnecessary. I've been through these kinds of projects before and they always fail and then I have to pick up the pieces.
Do: Hesitation, avoidance, outright subterfuge.	Feel: What happens if this works and my job totally changes? I'm not ready for that. I am not sure I have the skills to adapt to the change. I might have to find a different job.

The importance of the empathy maps isn't correctness, and it certainly isn't judgment - its awareness. It will bring to light the issues you will likely see as you move down the path of change.

Another way to think about this, and one I've seen in organizations, is the "Head, Heart, Hands" model. Like empathy maps, it focuses on the people affected by the change and only works if you engage all three: the head (thinking or rationality), the heart (feeling) and the hands (behaviors). The most prolific and seemingly well-adopted change model is ADKAR: Awareness, Desire, Knowledge, Ability, and Reinforcement. Originally created by Prosci founder Jeff Hiatt, it quickly identifies the five principles that organizations must consider before launching change management efforts.[7] One of the things I appreciate about the ADKAR model is its "journey over destination" approach. Many of the change efforts I've witnessed focus too much on the communication of the change, and too little on the process or how the change shifts over time. Any of these methods is a great place to start to remind yourself and your change team that disrupting data governance is about the people and the people need to be your focus.

As my conversation with Dan continued, I asked a question about change itself, the pace and how ubiquitous it is. With an echo of clarity, Dan simply stated: "Organizations are missing the human component in the pace of business." I started thinking about all the times I've worked on a change effort, and all the companies I've seen over the years and it occurred to me

---

[7] https://bit.ly/1qKvLyJ.

that I've not really seen any change effort done well. Sure, some have been done better than others, but full-scale change efforts, particularly ones that get to the heart of the organization's culture, are exceedingly difficult. I suspect that's because it is so much easier to focus on the items that you can check off from your project list. It's easy to check off tasks associated with technology. You can get servers online, install software, modify software, and fiddle with obscure checkboxes in the software until the cows come home. It feels like progress and, with traditional waterfall techniques, it looks like progress too. Trouble is, it's not where the real work is at and it's not where you'll find success either. It's just kicking the can down the street.

> "Everyone brings emotional baggage that doesn't fit in the overhead compartment."
>
> Dan Olson

The messy middle

Of course, a lot of change management is about communication, the how and when you do it. The challenges associated with communicating are different depending on your role in the organization. If you think about your organization as a triangle, at the very top are the executives. Next, are the middle managers and finally, at the base, the individual contributors. Communicating and cascading when you're an executive in charge of thousands of people looks and feels different than a middle manager that is responsible for two employees. The interesting thing is, there's a communication effort at the individual contributor level too, one that is often ignored. What do the individual contributors say to one another when the executives and managers are done sharing the message? That's an important piece of the puzzle and one that when ignored can imbue discontent and fear if not managed. The best person to get a hold of water-cooler talk is the middle manager, who is also in a position to manage up to the executives to help them understand what is being said at the individual contributor level. Especially, when that water-cooler talk has significantly impacted the change effort. That's not always easy in certain cultures though.

I remember a time when I was a middle manager in an organization that had gone through an enormous amount of change in a short span of time. There was a lot of executive turnover, some bad publicity, and a poorly managed reduction in force. People were upset, frustrated and fearful. The executives pulled all the people leaders together and tried to answer as many questions as possible. During a townhall-style panel discussion, a seeded question prompted an uncoached question from the audience: "How can I trust you when I've heard this before, and nothing has changed?" It was without a doubt the question on everyone's mind and thankfully someone was brave enough to ask it. Unfortunately, it's also a very difficult question to answer if it catches you off guard. That's the position many organizations are in now and executives must be prepared to address tough questions and concerns with more than just standard fodder. I cringe recalling how the executive in this particular situation responded, "I'd love to answer that, but we are out of time." I don't think I have to go into detail about how that was received by the employees in the room and the impact of the subsequent water-cooler conversations.

Hallmarks of a job well done

I'm always on the hunt for measurable success metrics. The ones that convey, beyond a reasonable doubt, you did what you said you were going to do. Sometimes the results are so obvious it's not that important to show the data, but I still like to be prepared. When it comes to change management, there was a part of me that wondered if irrefutable success metrics were even feasible. So, my last question to Dan was: how do you know when you're successful?

The calculation actually turned out to be pretty easy. You start with the organization's total spend on the initiative. For example, if you're implementing a big new system, like a customer relationship management (CRM) tool or an electronic health record (EHR), those systems are easily in the millions of dollars. Then, as in our example, you determine how much of the initiative's success is dependent on the utilization and adoption of the system. It plays out something like this: If the implementation of the new system costs the organization one million dollars and your goal is eighty percent adoption - that means that $800,000 is on the line. When you look at it like that, even a five percent budget for a change management effort, in this case, $50,000- is a small price to pay.

The hallmark of a successful change effort is *actually having a change plan*. When Dan shared that with me, I had a "Well, duh!" moment. In fact, this is backed up by data that Prosci collects. According to their website "…initiatives with excellent change management are six times more likely to meet objectives than those with poor change management." In addition, by moving from poor to fair change management increases the likelihood of meeting the objective three times![8]

Starting with the people first, being prepared to answer the hard questions, communicating and cascading messages, that's the work of the change agent. Then you must get up the next morning and do it again, and again. This is where the real effort lies. If the success criteria for a change management effort is

---

[8] https://bit.ly/2PTdAUy.

whether or not you planned for a change management effort, then I think it's time we start planning out this work, don't you? If you think you took this job because you like data and want to spend your days analyzing it, then data governance may not be right for you. This is a change agent job, pure and simple.

Simply complicated

We have established that disrupting data governance is something we need to do. After considering the people and the technology and the processes, we should be ready to start, right? Let's not underestimate how difficult it can be for data people to acknowledge that most data governance work exists within the fluid artistry of change management. We like balanced equations, reliable answers, and consistency of methods - yet here we are.

After working with so many clients, I'm rarely surprised by their responses toward transitioning to a data-driven culture. Once, I had a heart surgeon tell me that she couldn't understand *my* job; it seemed so hard. I thought she was kidding at first, but she wasn't. Trust me, heart surgery is more difficult and there is so much more on the line, but the idea that data and specifically data governance is almost too complicated to tackle is a common reaction. Einstein is credited with the quote; any idiot can make something complicated. It takes a genius to make it easy. I'm no genius (unless you ask my dad), but I was curious about the continuum of complexity. Specifically, are there levers that transition a task from hard to complicated to complex? Turns out, there kind of is. In the book "It's not complicated," author Rick Nason breaks down these differences to help leaders tackle bigger issues. In summary, the difference between something being complicated or complex is whether or not the pieces of the task can be broken out and dealt with in a logical manner. The one thing Nason offered that really resonated with me is the idea that we have to think about how we can *manage* big problems not how to solve them. We will never "solve" data governance. It is not a one and done exercise, but it *can* be broken apart into bite-sized efforts, and therefore doesn't need to be complex.

Almost all data work is a journey, not a destination. Focusing on managing the change toward modern data governance, rather than solving for the task will ensure success in your effort.

Plan the work...work the plan

Communication is the key part of your change management plan. In the appendix, you will find a sample communication plan for use as a starting point. Keep in mind that communication must be a two-way street. You can't just push out emails and think that you are communicating the change. If we follow the ADKAR model and maintain a consistent frequency of communication across different channels of communication, you're on firm ground to gain traction for your change.

One of the most critical things you will have to communicate is the nucleus of the idea that using data is good; even if it seems like that data might not be "right." Seeing it, using it and providing open channels for feedback, creates a system to continuously address the data issues that will inevitably arise. For too long we have rested this effort on the shoulders of small, over-wrought, isolated IT or analytics teams. If you want to create a true data culture, everyone must embrace the benefits of widespread use of data in day-to-day business, as well as acknowledge that we will find "bad" data and fix it, and that's okay because it's just part of the process.

One of the most difficult things ahead of you is convincing your analysts that this is a good idea. It's a natural instinct for analysts to dig their feet in, because you are taking away (in their mind) the work they have a lot of history and experience with. It may be some crazy, unscalable, manual effort that makes you question their sanity, but it is also the work that gets them the kudos and "data hero" status that keeps them around. Any change, but certainly a change that disrupts a person's routine can be deeply troubling.

Not all of them – in fact, probably only a few of them – will agree with you; you'll have to find a way to be okay with that. Pick a few to pioneer your data governance change. These analysts can be part of your broader group of data ambassadors, helping to protect and promote the use of the data assets. Second, you will have to select a few people that are data-savvy, but not analysts. Give them the data they have always wanted and then be there for the inevitable questions, challenges, and wins. Think of these efforts as pilot programs and when you do have wins or key lessons learned, use those as in your communication plan. Rationally winning over people with what others have done or seen in relevant context is a great place to start. But, remember the most important thing is to create a plan to manage the change.

Wrapping it up

The difficult truth about this is regardless of the type of data governance you want to do, traditional or modern; the work is in the change management. Be well prepared by creating a communication plan, gaining champions throughout the organization and creating a high degree of visibility to the work you do. Communicate constantly, helping everyone from the top leadership to the front-line staff see that they have a role in governance.

CHAPTER 5

Data Quality

I have a confession to make: I have a tattoo. Okay, I have five tattoos, but one of them has recently become more relevant to me. Let me take you back twenty years, to 1997. I had just started my master's program and on the very first day of class, my professor (the incomparable Lou Milanesi, Ph.D.) wrote two things on the whiteboard:

"There is no such thing as a free lunch" and "X = T + E"

The first one was self-explanatory; the second though, for us rookie grad students, required some explanation. Simply: the observed score (X) equals the true score (T), plus error (E). In layman's terms, the key takeaway is this: whatever you do with data, consider the possibility of error. This resonated with me deeply. This relatively simple concept is at the heart of applied statistics; it drove most of my education for those two years. But there was something else – something almost philosophical – inherent in that simple X = T + E equation. I ruminated on this idea so much that one day, on little more than a whim and a few extra dollars, I finally stopped at the tattoo shop that was nearest my favorite watering hole. With just a couple of characters' worth of ink, I permanently committed to this simple idea: in whatever you do, consider the possibility of error.

Fast-forward a few decades and I sometimes forget the tattoo is even there. But the concept remains strong; in all things we do, we should consider the possibility of error, shouldn't we? And as someone who is permanently attached to the philosophy, it's high time I dust it off and see if it still has legs.

Error in data is ubiquitous. In an existential crisis, it's almost as if data isn't data without some level of error in it, at least at the macro level. We spend a lot of time hand wringing about data quality, yet when we find ourselves in a time crunch, our quality assurance procedures are often the first things we skimp on. When there's time to think and work rationally, people generally choose "good" from the triad of "Good, Fast or Cheap" because they feel it's the right choice. But in the real world, where time is short and the pressure is high, fast has become the default.

In almost every organization I have ever worked, whether as a consultant or as an employee, someone will tell me that the data quality is a problem. Scroll through any social media trail about data and eventually, you will trip on a data quality thread. Good data quality is imperative to almost anything we do in machine learning and artificial intelligence. Anecdotal stats abound with the time people take "cleaning the data." Just ask any analyst how much time they spend cleaning the data before they can use it and most of them will tell you it's more than fifty percent for any given project, and more often aligns with the 80/20 rule.

The Data Quality Imperative

Let's just all agree we need the data to be of high quality, shall we? It might be the last thing we agree on, but we can agree on that much. Good data quality leads to better, faster and more scalable analytic solutions. If we can't claim good data quality, then what's the point of creating a data governance program? Yet we find ourselves in an interesting predicament. We all agree it's important, but in terms of *how* to get there, I see a gap the size of the Grand Canyon.

This chapter almost didn't make it into the book. I was finished writing when I was forced to pause and reconsider. I was documenting recommendations for data warehouse testing for a client and I wanted to include reinforcing literature from third parties. My focus was specifically on *what* you test in a data warehouse and *how* you test it. I turned to my good friend Google and sat dumbfounded. The lack of actionable content on the pragmatic work on data quality in a data warehouse is paltry. It's embarrassing for us as an industry that is so well established, for a topic such as data quality in a data warehouse to be nearly non-existent.

Now, before you come at me on Twitter with reference links, I know there's content out there on this product or that product and consultants (me included) have blogs on the subject of data quality. I included a number of books in the appendix as well. But what I was looking for was an actual example that a rookie data warehouse architect could use as a starting point for implementing his or her own repeatable, scalable methodology for data quality. Suddenly, it occurred to me that the reason data analysts spend so much time on data quality is that it seems like no one else has.

This has also been reflected in my personal experiences. I have encountered more than one data warehouse that had virtually no data quality processes associated with it, except for maybe row counts. It's important to note, however, that there is a high level of academic content on data quality standards. What seems to be missing is something in between high-level academic fodder and articles on the specific quality tests. This chapter will explore the data quality challenges we face in areas in the context of data governance, and more specifically getting the (high quality) data out to our average end-users.

In all likelihood, some of the lack of content on data quality procedures is related to the overwhelming nature of the subject itself, particularly for a modern data warehouse. The volume and veracity of data that comes at us every day is like a tsunami. With our stakeholders and end-users already impatiently waiting, are we really going to tell them that the data has to pass five to six tests before they can have it? Or, the tests that we have built into the transformation code starts to slow down the loading processes. Scenarios abound with issues related to how you implement data quality into a data warehouse.

> "The road to hell is paved with good intentions."
>
> Proverb

Let's organize this thing and take all the fun out of it, shall we? First, a definition: "Data has quality if it satisfies the requirements of its intended use. It lacks quality to the extent that it does not satisfy the requirement." (Olson, Jack. *Data Quality: The Accuracy Dimension*. 2003. Morgan Kaufman). I don't care if you have the smartest people, the best technology, cutting-edge methods and a bottomless cup of coffee, you can't measure intention. Intention does not have a baseline for comparison. It is a hope, a target, usually only known to the person - or in our case, the analyst.

I am a begrudging former data analyst. I can tell you from the years I spent as a mouse jockey that the intention I had when I started an analysis and the end result were often two different things. I can also tell you that if we are truly doing data exploration, the intention should be "I don't know yet." I can understand what Jack Olson was getting at, yet intention is not what we should measure data quality against - it's actually *context.* It's a judgment of fitness of purpose that can and should be objective. But here's the challenge, and it's the same quandary we find ourselves in with data governance: how do we hit a moving target? Context and fit-for-purpose *changes* as the situations change. In a standard measurement situation, I would create a baseline and measure the current against it to get the delta. But if the baseline changes (our context) how can I objectively assess the delta?

What we test

It is broadly known that there are six aspects of data quality. There are a lot of articles on these dimensions; I prefer one from the CDC based on the DAMA UK work. Depending on the article you read, the dimensions may have slightly different names, but they are fundamentally the same:

- Completeness
- Uniqueness
- Timeliness
- Validity
- Accuracy
- Consistency[9]

---

[9] https://bit.ly/2UfxSut.

You can, in all reasonableness, create standard tests for these dimensions and apply them to your data warehouse. Though what you will find is that it does not address the gap we have explored: context and fit-for-purpose. Accuracy attempts to get close with a definition often referencing the need for the data to reflect the "real world," but it does not address how people *want* to use the data.

The definition we can apply for "context" in our six dimensions of data quality is: "The data has a standard, approved definition with an associated algorithm." This should reflect the business context within which the data lives. It provides us a standard, an algorithm, an objective testing baseline and the ability to look at it and say, "No, I'm not using that definition." I've said this a few times, but there's a big difference between how a nurse manager defines a patient and how a finance manager defines a patient and for good reason. The intention of the purpose of these two roles is vastly different. The other benefit of adding "context" as one of the dimensions of good data quality is the ability to apply that as a standard test to the data warehouse. The traditional versions of data governance attempted to do this often, and when it is achieved it does advance the standards of data quality coming out of the data warehouse.

Unfortunately, context isn't enough to fully address the challenges we have with data quality. The trouble we find ourselves in when creating standard definitions as part of our data governance efforts is that the enforced standard definition may be in conflict with the intended use of the data. Or, an alternative way of thinking about it: fit-for-purpose (FFP)[10].

As an analyst, there will always be reasons why the data needs to be reviewed and "cleaned," even in cases where good data quality methods have been applied. There's a certain *je ne sais quoi* or indefinable quality that is commonplace for analysts to look for in a dataset. A sort of "sniff test" to assess a dataset's ability to address the question(s) they're attempting to answer. It's not uncommon at this point for analysts to take the dataset and begin a first round of simple analysis, thinking through all potential variables.

This is also the point where the analyst may choose to not follow the standard definition of a metric because it does not fit the purpose. The dataset assessment should identify the minimum fields to which the analyst must apply their algorithms, and sometimes the analyst doesn't know what these are until they are deep into exploration. There is an art to analyzing data, particularly when open questions like "why is our volume so low?" are presented. Off the cuff analysts will know what data fields are required, but until they fully explore the data and the

---

[10] Quantifying the Effect of Data Quality on the Validity of an eMeasure Johnson et al. Appl Clin Inform 2017;8:1012–1021.

questions they won't know what they are looking for or need of the data.

Earlier we used the example of the "patient," which is defined differently by people in two different roles (the patient manager and the finance manager). Often the definition of a patient is dependent on time; analysts consider whether there was a person in a bed at midnight on some given day. That temporal definition helps finance managers ensure they can charge for a full day's stay, and it helps the nurse manager plan for staffing.

The trouble begins when we go any deeper than that surface definition. When we start to ask questions like "Why was volume low on that unit compared to last year." What about the scenario in which the finance manager has to use risk scores to forecast how many patients the hospital will have and how sick those patients might be so they can plan for how much financial risk the organization can manage? What about the type of staffing a nurse manager with lots of complicated patient's needs? We must take into consideration not just the number of staff, but also the level of staff (RN vs. LPN). Throw in the work of infectious disease; they actually care less about the "patient" status and a whole lot more about whether or not the individual was on a particular unit at a particular time. You can see how quickly a standard definition falls apart. Any of these data would have held its completeness, validity, accuracy, consistency, timeliness and uniqueness. It just failed the fit-for-purpose test.

While context is something that we can add to a data warehouse testing methodology, fit-for-purpose may always be the one thing that a *person* (e.g., an analyst) has to assess.

How we test

Now that we have expanded our list of *what* to test (adding context and fit for purpose), we must determine *how* we test. I highly recommend reading the DataOps Cookbook from DataKitchen. It does a nice job of framing data quality tests in a DataOps way. The assumption is you will be using some type of agile practice. The process you choose doesn't necessarily have to be DataOps.

Let us pause here to make an important distinction. Just because we know we have to test for validity, for instance, doesn't mean we know exactly *how* to execute that test. To make this determination, we turn to the traditional best practices in data quality assurance. Examples of tests used in quality assurance are:

- Unit Testing
- Integration Testing
- Functional Testing
- Regression Testing

The first step is unit testing, which tests the smallest incremental pieces of the deliverable. It's often done during the development of the code by the developer, but it is recommended that another set of eyes examine that code before you ship it. Integration testing focuses on the interactions between code packages; it looks for integrations or interactions that break one another. Functional tests feed data into our code package and assess the output, searching for unanticipated results based on the code. Finally, regression tests are specific to changes in code, attempting to isolate the changes to ensure they produce the expected results. Now, we look to combine the type of tests we need to run and how we execute tests to ensure we test the dimensions of data quality. First, we have to consider the different layers of a modern data warehouse: integration, staging, the data repository, and an analytic sandbox. Not all tests are critical across all of these environmental layers. For each of these layers there are different tests:

Table 1: The "*What*" Tests

Data Layers	Types of Tests
Integration	Completeness, Conformity, Format checks
Staging	Consistency, Conformity, Accuracy, Integrity, Timeliness
Repository	Completeness, Consistency, Conformity, Accuracy, Integrity, Timeliness, Context
Sandbox	Integrity, Timeliness, Fit-for-purpose

The second section lists what tests you use to test each aspect of data quality based on each of the layers in a modern data platform and the phase you're in; building, automating or monitoring. These are just suggestions based on what we have reviewed in this chapter. These tables are exactly what I was looking for when I started that Google search. Modify these to reflect your own environments and the tests that you complete today. You can also find a combined table in the appendix.

Table 2: The "*How*" Tests

Data Layers	Build	Automate	Monitor
Integration	Unit Functional (Regression)	Integration Functional	Performance Functional Conformity Completeness
Staging	Unit Functional (Regression)	Integration Functional	Performance Functional -Conformity -Consistency -Accuracy -Integrity -Timeliness
Repository	Unit Functional (Regression)	Integration Functional	Performance Functional -Conformity -Consistency -Accuracy -Integrity -Timeliness - Context
Sandbox	Functional (Regression)	Functional	Performance

There are just more "hooks"

Even if we have the most thoroughly tested data warehouse, with all six dimensions tested if we add context and fit-for-purpose as two new aspects of data quality, no analysts are off the hook from data testing. Thankfully, it is relatively easy to make sure your testing process runs as efficiently and as smoothly as possible. To do this, your first task is to create a vigorous and automated testing schedule for the data environments. Automating as many of the tests as possible will alleviate some of the pressure. Next, create a solid plan for context and fit-for-purpose testing. Context testing of the data will change as WD's change. Presenting the quality testing in an easy to understand manner, such as a dashboard will help to create a tight alliance between the analytics team and the quality assurance team.

There is no such thing as 100% data quality. It just can't exist. There's too much data and too many ways to use the data. What we should strive for, and something that's much more feasible is using the data and then talking about how we used the data so that we can all understand the data better. Better understanding leads to better outcomes, but only if we actively confer with each other.

As the saying goes, the juice has to be worth the squeeze and sometimes (keenly true in healthcare today) we just assume that the work is worth it. Not all data is created equal. Just as we will not govern every variable in your data environments, it's not feasible to manage every cell of data in your ever-increasing data environments. When I spoke with Steve Johnson on the topic of data quality, he shared a nugget that I wrote down on a sticky (if you saw my office you would see how sticky notes run my life): "Data quality depends on how people want to use the data." As we have seen, we can't measure intention, but we can find and measure what we know definitively to be true. Understanding there is a difference between the two, and managing for that difference, is a great approach to data quality standards.

The applicability of my tattoo, X=T+E, is compelling since it is the primary basis for classic test theory. That said, there is not a one to one comparison between testing a data environment for every possible analysis and the attempt to control the variability of error in correlations, but there is *some* relationship (see what I did there?).

Wrapping it up

Data quality tests are the canary in the coal mine of your data governance processes. If you have good data governance processes the data quality tests should look stable. Without any quality tests, or without the ability to communicate the quality tests you lose your early warning system for governance.

CHAPTER 6

Putting it all Together

Congratulations, you made it to the end. In this chapter, we will put together all of the things we have learned and create a framework for implementation. The tools and methods outlined here will be a valuable resource as you begin your journey. The appendix includes helpful supporting content that isn't directly tied to implementation, but important enough to include.

In order to increase our odds of success, we will jump around a bit between our pillars of people, process, technology and culture. The order in which you do things is important, and I will include a note if steps can be moved due to constraints that are sometimes difficult to control (i.e. hiring). I recommend you take the time to review this entire chapter before starting, sort of like a recipe, read it through once and then get started.

Trust, value and a broken chain

Before we officially break off into implementation mode, we need to address the issue that has put us in this position in the first place. In the first chapter, the issue of broken trust was outlined. Of all of the research I did on governance in organizations, this was probably the one thing that I kept coming back to, broken trust.

It's very difficult to define trust, and even more difficult to "fix" it once it's broken. While we have tried our best, the gap between the outputs (actions) of governance and the outcomes (results) are significant. We have historically put a great degree of effort in, with people and software, but are unable to show in a *very tangible way* the outcome. In Simon Sinek's book, "*Start with Why*," he defines trust as the transference of value, and as I read that I realized that is why trust is so often brought up in a governance context.

We fail to consistently provide VALUE. Sometimes it's because the value is not clear. Take for example creating standard definitions. Picking one definition and forcing an entire organization to use *only* that definition is not the transference of value. It's telling a number of people throughout the organization that how they use data isn't relevant. Would you trust someone if they told you that? Sometimes we claim the value through risk avoidance, such as regulatory concerns. The language we use in these situations often makes a bad governance situation worse. A fear-based set of hyperbolic language geared toward action and motivation, almost by definition, breaks down trust. Here's a good example: when I spoke with people about this work and the need to democratize access to data, I got a lot of "But this is healthcare, you're going to kill someone!" Folks, that's not true. It's hyperbole and dangerous because it puts everyone on their heels. It's meant to intimidate you into thinking that there are no other ways. I would even argue that the way we do the work now is likely doing as much, if not more, harm than giving people exposure to the data so we can all make better, safer and more informed decisions. This type of language does more to break down trust than to build it up. Somewhere in the pit of your stomach, when you hear statements like that the reaction is guttural. Our reactions are "you're right, I don't want to touch this" or "BS, and now I trust you even less." Trust has to be at the cornerstone of your new data governance movement. Which means that you have to focus on the transference of value.

People first

We have to start with the people. It's critical to not only ensure you have the resources but also take the time to gain alignment among them. The decision to improve data governance obviously starts with someone. For illustration purposes, let's say that a Chief Data Officer has identified this as a risk or an issue and starts the process of re-framing data governance. The first thing a CDO must do is to hire or promote a leader of the new data governance, someone who will be responsible for the day-to-day operations of the governance function. In chapter two, we included some job descriptions, and this first juncture is where you may choose to seek out a lead data (governance) ambassador.

If you have to hire externally, that's going to take a while, so I'd encourage the CDO to use the time wisely by starting the change management plan. Ideally, the CDO will also work with a peer or two to ensure solid executive support. Once the lead data ambassador is hired, the first step for she or he will be convening an in-service meeting to get the ball rolling. I call it an "in-service" because, by definition, it allows for those actively engaged in a profession to lend their expertise to your cause without shifting their main focus.

Every attendee of the in-service is an expert in their own right, coming together for the betterment of data in your organization. Below is a sample in-service agenda and if you remember, chapter two talks about each area in more detail. This in-service should include the lead data ambassador, the CDO and a peer of the CDO such as the COO, CFO or CIO. If you have an enlightened CISO, including them would be beneficial too. If your CISO is very focused on the protection part and constantly tells you why this won't work, the in-service may not be the time to include them. It's up to you. Of course, you will have to win them over at some point, but including them in negotiating scope and budget may not be the best place to start.

The in-service will likely take three to four hours and it is *not* negotiable. If you receive a lot of pushback on the amount of time it will take, or people decline to attend, stop here and do some "managing up."

If your executives aren't fully on board, you have to take the time to make sure they are really ready to support the effort. This is particularly true for those organizations that don't have a CDO (or a CDO in title only). If you have a CDO, it's less impactful, but still important to have other executives committed to the effort. When the doors to the board room shut and you can't be there to support your effort, your budget might get cut before you even start.

Use the "head, heart, hands" framework we discussed in chapter five to help them jump on the bandwagon. Be well prepared with value statements from your organization, sections of this book or check out routetwentyfive.com to see how other organizations have been successful.

It is possible to break up the day into two parts if schedules are tight. Gently remind them that three to four hours for this meeting, plus a few additional meetings throughout the year, is just eight hours of support for an essential corporate asset. Don't proceed without it. You won't get far.

In-service agenda

Topic	Duration	Leader? Comments?
Scope		
Budget		
Schedule		
Success Metrics		
Roles: Sponsor Leader Average user		

> There is an exception to the "get your executives on board" directive. If you work at a large, multinational, federated organization it may not be possible to have more than one executive on board. If this is your situation, there's still value in tackling governance for your department. Just make sure that you still have your leadership in the know. Small to mid-sized companies will be better positioned with a top-down/bottom-up approach. These larger conglomerates will have to build their efforts one group at a time.

Once the in-service is complete there are a couple of things that have to move forward at the same time: communication and hiring. Communication is a key component of the change management plan and critically important to the success of the effort. This will not be the only time you will communicate about data governance; you will repeat yourself more times than you could imagine, but this first time will be the memo that changes everything.

Last year I was traveling for a conference when a friend asked if I would do a workshop for the data teams in their organization while I was in town. I happily accepted, because I like doing workshops and helping teams get over obstacles. The obstacle in this instance was multi-layered, but most pointedly stemmed from having no less than three separate teams supporting data and analytics, and they all reported up through different executives. It was easy to see how quickly things could get confusing. The teams had done a lot of work, including discussing the issue of disconnectedness. As I stood in front of them, it quickly became obvious that I was really there to orchestrate the next step. I was there to help them overcome the obstacle: the need to be brought together as one team. The impacted executives were in the room and at the first break the CIO came up to me and said: "What if we just had all the teams report to one person?" They had all come to the same conclusion, and as a group were more ready than they even knew.

We reconvened after the break and I broached the subject that I knew was on everyone's mind. The biggest question was who supported the transition to one team and who did not. Then as they started to realize they were all on the same page, the CIO said, "It's time to write the life-changing memo." And that was the beginning. The CIO understood that communicating the change was the first order of the day.

Your own version of a life-changing memo has to be based on what you know about your organization. Start with why, remember to appeal to their heads and hearts, and give them some things to expect. It's also valuable at this point to give them some steps: ask them to talk to the lead data ambassador or CDO if they have questions, or if they're interested in helping. Furthermore, this life-changing memo should be just one of many; plan to message early and often. Adopting a change management plan will help keep your messaging consistent and relevant.

At the same time, you should be creating job descriptions and a career trajectory for the resources that will fill your new data governance initiative. Ideally, you will partner with your human resources department, because it may take some effort to either create a job family or re-engineer your analytics job family. This can be a parallel effort or if you see it as a more integrated effort (i.e. analysts and ambassadors are interchangeable) you may just need to re-title some folks and be on your way. Either way, you will want to take a few days to think this through, make sure you hire the right way and have a plan to allow people to excel at their jobs. Although you'll likely feel the pressure to move as quickly as possible try to be mindful that you are laying an important foundation for your staff.

Once you have hired or promoted the roles you need, based on the scope you have identified, you're ready to roll. Communication should be disseminated as close to this time as possible so as to not get too people excited or anger them for moving too fast without any notification. It's a tricky balance but more communication is better than less communication.

Your scope should have been negotiated during your in-service, and as a part of this, you should have also identified your success metrics. You need to begin with the end in mind, and make sure that everything you do after this point is measurable. If you can't measure it and tie it to tangible and accepted business success, then you have to re-negotiate. Keep in mind that these can and should shift. As you restart your data governance effort with this modern twist, your focus or areas of importance may look different than they do now.

These ratios of importance were part of the interviews I held while researching for this book. Each person I interviewed was asked this question "If we re-frame data governance as a focus on data usage, ensuring the quality of the data within the context set by governance and relying on our internal partnerships for data protection, how would you assign importance. While certainly not a statistically significant methodology, the interviewees placed the majority emphasis on the usage with a great degree of swing for the remaining three.

Importance of New Data Governance Principles

Topic	% Importance
Increasing Usage of Data Assets	50%
Quality of Data	25%
Data Lineage (increase visibility)	15%
Protection	10%

Protection used to be at the top of this list but is now relegated to the last in importance. Not because it's not critical, but because you now have a partner that can help you operationalize it. Your InfoSec group should be involved in the determination of the success metrics for the protection aspect of data governance.

With your success metrics in one hand and your change management plan in the other (wait, that can't be right, how do you hold your coffee?) you are ready to go. Schedule the touchpoints you've agreed to with your key stakeholders far in advance. It seems simple enough, but calendars can be crazy. In agile terms that is your backlog, grooming, and retro.

One of the key elements of Modern Data Governance (MDG) is our method of combining traditional data governance councils, with the use of agile methods. In addition, most organizations need the ability to create a modular framework that can scale up or down depending on the volume and variety of additional strategic projects that rely on data. Agile and councils or committees are like oil and water, but in any form of data governance, we need the business context and expertise that these groups bring to the table. In MDG we still have these experts participate but as on-demand subject-matter-experts. Think of them like your adjunct product owners, they help guide the product (in our case data) to delivery.

The Workflow

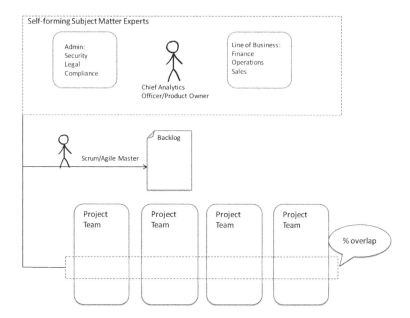

Briefly, from the top, you have two groups of people (or in traditional governance, they would have been our committees) with shared organizational responsibility that may or may not formally meet. The first is a line of business (LOB) data governance group that allows you to create standard data definitions, data quality standards, and usage criteria. The other council, which we will refer to as the data governance administration, is dedicated to the creation of policies and procedures for compliance, privacy, and security. In this framework, your governance administration group will provide you with their requirements that you have to fulfill. The difference is they then are not at the table listening to meetings about how to define data. Think about these two groups like functional and non-functional requirements. They are equally important but need to be managed separately. The glue that holds them together is your data governance leader. You need someone in this role who is accountable and can drive things forward. There is nothing agile or responsive about lots of committees or councils.

From the bottom up, imagine those long rectangles to be your annual projects. You can add more or remove them, they can switch out, but this is how you start to integrate your persistent council with your reality of project-based work. Working groups are assigned to participate in these projects. Their function is to document and identify efforts that overlap in terms of data, such as customer problems that some or all of the projects share. Whether that is definitions, usage, quality, or risk, their job is to put it into a backlog. Backlog items can be added from the persistent councils as well. Things like data masking or operationalizing definitions for standard usage can all be combined into one backlog.

Depending on the size and scope of your team, the working group and the agile data team could be one and the same. A working group is an on-demand group, existing only when there are projects that either directly or peripherally impact the data. If you're large enough, the agile data team will persist, and there will always be work associated with governance.

A list of stuff to do

Now that brings us to our next topic: creating your backlog. Using DataOps principles for our deployment of MDG will help to quickly deliver the minimally valuable product (MVP). A DataOps approach is a good fit here because this is a journey, not a destination; you won't ever really stop data governance efforts.

A sample backlog is available in the appendix. For our purposes here, we will only review a few things that would typically go into the backlog. A backlog is simply a list of stuff to do. Remember back to the process chapter, when we reviewed the DataOps Manifesto by Chris Bergh's company DataKitchen (Which was named a "Cool Vendor" by Gartner as I was writing this book!) and how to adapt it for MDG – now we will put it into practice.

In full disclosure, as I attempted to write this section, I hit a bit of writer's block. I struggled to describe a backlog as anything more than a list of stuff to do, as I did in the title. Thankfully, I stumbled upon the most eloquent description of a backlog I've ever seen. As they say, don't reinvent the wheel, and I will absolutely give appropriate credit.

"The product owner focuses on the "what" and the development team on the "how." The product backlog should be a list of customer problems to be solved or "jobs to be done." An item on the backlog should not detail the production solution…that comes later. This is simply a placeholder for a conversation to be had. Once the development team begins working the problem, they meet with the customer to better understand and determine a solution.

They may pivot to a different solution at any point during the sprint, but the goal remains the same. This means the sprint backlog will evolve throughout this sprint as the development teams learn more." - Robert Weidner

In the grand scheme of things, I consider myself to be an agile newbie and, occasionally, I read something like this and have one of those aha moments – this was one of them. It makes perfect sense, it's agile, of course the solution and even the backlog itself will change! Maybe you don't share in my excitement for this revelation, maybe you're already an agile expert, but I think it's an important perspective to have when applying agile to MDG. Think about the power of a data governance backlog when you focus on a customer's problem and create a series of backlog items as placeholders to solve it. Let's start with one we all know and love: the executives all have different definitions of customers, members, patients, employees, visits, products, etc. I think you get the picture.

Data Governance Ops (DGOps) a beginning

As I wrapped up my research on data governance and specifically how to improve it, I found myself struggling with what data governance is at its core, both for the broader data and analytics industry and for the individual organization. I know what it's not: it's not a tool to threaten, it's not a set of documents that gather dust, and it's not the veritable "other" bucket for analytic work. Yet so often we treat it as these things or worse.

Recently, I spoke with a CIO about data governance and his reaction was immediate. I'm paraphrasing, but roughly it was "Ugh, data governance. We've tried that so many times and then the person that does data governance leaves and it's over. It's worse than boiling the ocean. It's boiling the ocean one cup at a time while arguing about the kind of algae is in the cup."

The reason we struggle so much with governance is that at the end of the day governance is about building trust. There is almost no value in the way we have historically done data governance. That stops today, right here with you and me and a little thing I'm calling DGOps. Yes, I'm borrowing from DevOps and my friends at DataKitchen's framework for DataOps. It is short for Data Governance Operations and it will completely reframe how we do data governance.

DGOps creates a subtle but powerful shift in how we design, discuss and implement the functions that equate to data governance. Like all agile frameworks, we value individual interactions over processes and tools. We define data governance as having these four attributes: Increasing usage, improved data quality, documented data lineage and protection of data assets. Each of these provides direct, tangible value back to the organization by ensuring a framework to democratize access to data. In other words, if these things are all in place, anyone in the organization can use data without concern of different, wrong, or poor-quality data.

The DGOps tenets

- We value the **usage** of the data over control of the asset.

- Our priority is to increase the usage of data throughout the organization by creating a **responsive** system of governance.

- **Transparency** of the data, from source, to its target and everywhere in between.

- We must **communicate** what we've learned and what we know frequently.

- **Quality** is the result of good governance. Our focus is to create a resilient system that improves the quality of the data.

- We recognize the importance of **security** and **privacy** by forming a happy alliance with our InfoSec and Compliance partners.

- We seek to **operationalize** data governance efforts in a tangible way into the data environments.

- We encourage **questions** about the data because that means we're increasing usage.

- Our intent is to focus on **progress** not perfection in all things data. Allow for iterations to constantly improve the data, definitions, and quality.

- **Self-forming** teams build better systems. Focus on the "what" and let the teams figure out the how.

- Start small, with **simple** achievable steps toward governed data that imbues usage and value to the organization.

I love this DevOps definition from the Agile Admin website:[11]

> "[DevOps is] a cross-disciplinary community of practice dedicated to the study of building, evolving and operating rapidly-changing resilient systems at scale." It's attributed to Jez Humble.

Communicate, communicate, communicate

In the world of real estate, the saying is "location, location, location." For data governance, it's all about communication, communication, communication. It is sometimes boring and repetitive work. If you hate it as much as I do, find someone with an affinity for the relationship management aspect of data governance and ask him or her for assistance. You can't underestimate its importance. Without a concerted, thoughtful and thorough plan to communicate about the change in data governance, and specifically the "why" of the change, all the work will fall on unappreciative deaf ears.

Before I ever considered writing this book, I was working as the Director of Analytics at a hospital. For reasons best left untold, I left that job at the beginning of 2019 and took the leap of faith to start my own venture. Shortly after that, I was confronted

---

[11] https://bit.ly/2aL34PV.

with the opportunity to write another book, this book. And in all honesty, I wasn't sure if I had another one in me. I'm still not sure I do (and yes, I know this is the last chapter), but creating content for this book required me to reflect heavily on my tenure at the hospital and I realized something. I had failed at spectacularly at communicating. The topic I keep harping on as being so critical. Don't get me wrong, I did communicate... at the beginning. When I first started and even a fair amount into my second year, but after that? Almost nothing. I have a truckload of excuses and lots of rationale. Some of it may even be legitimate, but I'm going to get real with you and admit that the truth is, I got bored with the message. I was tired of repeating myself. Exhausted by the constant "too much detail" or "not enough detail." It was an unending battle of calendars and will, and I simply gave up. I focused on the things I knew I could easily do. I'm not proud of it. They deserved better. I deserved better.

I did some soul searching and thought back to the point when I stopped communicating. Why did I make those choices? What I realized is something that many of these types of projects have in common: a movie. "Field of Dreams" was released in 1989 and starred Kevin Costner. I'm reasonably sure I've never seen the movie, but then again, I could have slept through it on a date, which is completely plausible. The movie's most famous line is the one that haunts almost every person in the data industry: "build it and they will come." Even though nowadays it's common sense that building data initiatives require a more sophisticated, long-term strategy, the if-you-build-it criticism still haunts many data warehouse teams. Often said as a result of not including the business on the project. The only way to avoid it is to have a way to keep connected to the business with a comprehensive and persistent communication plan.

It is easy to communicate the need for change when the project is new, and people are excited. It's easy when you haven't yet been beaten down, day after day, week after week, with the reality of the work. If you manage staff, then you have that to contend with as well. Pretty soon you look up and it's been months since you've talked with anyone outside of your team. When you do communicate to them your energy is gone and they pick up on it, convinced the project will fail. So, you stop communicating and figure the faster you get it done, the better off everyone will be. Then soon enough, there's the perception and/or reality that you've built it and expect that to come use it.We did communicate. We just stopped. But the lesson I have learned is that you can never stop communicating about the change. Even if you've said it a hundred times, you can't stop. You must keep saying it in slightly different ways to the same people, over and over. Even if you're exhausted and beaten down by an average Thursday, you can't stop. Make a plan, prepare key messages, find others that can help, and make sure that *not one week goes by* without some type of message going out about not only what you are doing, but WHY.

In the appendix, you will find a sample communication plan that weaves together the change management efforts we reviewed in chapter four. In every communication, you should frame it in the change management ADKAR with a heavy dose of Why, What, When, Where, How and How much. In an effort to not completely overwhelm yourself with the communication portion of the job, each quarter you should write enough messages for the following quarter. They should include updated references to where the project is at and a call to action to let the readers know how they can participate.

The tech

I doubt you need more software. In the average organization, the software has become like space junk, floating around, totally useless. You know it's bad, but you don't know what you're supposed to do about it. I have always been an advocate for a "wait and see" approach to technology. Hire the right people. Focus on putting together an efficient process. Finally, ask whether software can solve problems that competent people and clean processes can't. I elaborated a great deal in the technology chapter about how radically different tech is today in the data governance space. We finally have some compelling options that give us access, lineage, and transparency to all the data – not just the data in the environment you happen to actively work in.

The advice from chapter four to tread lightly on software acquisition is still relevant, though. I have seen too many data governance efforts start with a metadata tool, only to fail when they realize that metadata has no value without business context. It is so easy to implement software and claim you did something. Make sure any tools you select follow the tenets of DGOps and can deliver tangible value to increase usage of the data asset.

Realistically, tech is the last thing you will focus on after you tackle the bigger issues of people, processes, and culture. And you don't need me to tell you how to implement software. If you are using agile methods (more specifically, DGOps), your on-demand agile teams should help with tool selection. Create definitions and design algorithms, then test them for transparent consumption from the data catalog of your choice. If you start with a well-defined business problem, have the right people in place and follow agile methods, it will feel like all the pieces of the puzzle have fallen into place.

Wrapping it all up

We've come to this point in data governance because we've recognized throughout these pages that the way we have historically defined data governance hasn't changed in two decades but *everything* about data has changed. Democratizing data in your organization to gain insights and create value is critical to the long term success of analytic efforts. Yet data governance, specifically the traditional method of data governance, has not truly allowed you to democratize access to data. But that's exactly what we must realize, that data governance, and democratizing access to data, are two sides of the same coin. The first thing we need to do is to redefine what governance means to our organization: increasing usage, improving data quality, data lineage, and protection of the asset.

Our leadership should take an active role in ranking the importance of these four categories, another important distinction in the new data governance. Advocate first, knowing that the process to get to democratizing data means issues will be found, and that's just part of the process of increasing insights and usage. Data governance is no longer about stopping people from using the data, it's about creating a fertile environment in which the entire organization has a high degree of trust in data.

The tangible result of improved data governance efforts is improved data quality. Quality must be everyone's job because we have too much data to ever be able to govern it all with just analytic or data teams. If increasing usage results in people seeing more data, then the odds of more data issues being brought to light increases. Our new data governance focus helps us understand that when you identify issues with the data, you actually stand a chance of fixing more and more data. The more you fix the more people will trust and use it. You are creating an engine in which there's a high degree of transparency and trust which elicits value to your organization. It's time to work together in data governance to increase quality in our data assets.

When the people in your organization look at a report or an analysis, they should recognize that they are in fact acting as data stewards. If they find issues the goal is not to blame the person, system or process, but rather to bring forward the data quality issues so they can be fixed. Data isn't wrong, it's just data. When you thank people for finding issues in the data you fundamentally change the interaction between who uses the data and the people that "govern" the data. We want you to use the data because it's not feasible to do this work alone, we must do it together. The more you do this the faster the engine goes. When you democratize data this way people see the changes, they understand the challenges and that's how data-driven cultures begin.

I believe the work we do in data is like a road trip. It's about the journey and all that we learn on it, not the destination. There is no end to data governance and the challenges it will bring but there is too much at stake not to try – so just try. If data is considered an asset at your company but there's still a lot of fear around using it, just try. If your data governance efforts have failed to produce effective processes, just try. If doing it the same way feels like some version of an endlessly repeating loop, just try. If you try and you ultimately don't like the way MDG or DGOps works, at least you will have learned something that will make your next efforts better. After all, that's all any of us can hope for: leaving our organizations better than we found them.

Marketing and Communications Plan

[Company Name Here]

[Address 1]

[Address 2]

[Telephone]

[Company Website]

Revision History

Version	Author	Date

Corporate Mission:

[Insert your corporate mission here]

Program Objective:

[Insert Program Objective here]

Program Audience

Communication Plan

Communication Type	Audience	Timeline

Competitive Landscape

Marketing Objectives

What is the goal of marketing activities?

The goal of the marketing plan is to

- [Goal 1]
- [Goal 2]
- [Goal 3]

Sample activities…

Activity	Objective	Timeline	Success Parameters
Book Club	Broadly share the mission & vision of Analytics to all stakeholders	Quarterly	Moderate Participation
Analytics Awards	Broadly share the mission & vision of Analytics to all stakeholders	Annually	Minimum of 8 submissions
Monthly Update (brown bag)	Share Status Updates of the Analytics Program Build Out	Monthly	5 attendees or more
Newsletter	Broadly share the mission & vision of the Analytics program to all stakeholders. Share successes and updates	Every Other Month	Link Accessed at least 8 times
Speaker Series	Broadly share the mission & vision of the analytics to all stakeholders	Every Other Month	Moderate Participation
Open House	Share updates and successes of the Analytics Program	Between each phase of the project	Moderate Participation

Analytics Mission & Vision Statements

Mission Statement:

Vision Statement:

The What and How of Tests

Where	Integration Layer	Staging Area	Data Repository	Analytic Sandbox
What do you test for?				
Type of test	Completeness* i.e. row counts Conformity Format checks	Consistency Conformity Accuracy* Integrity Timeliness	Completeness* Consistency Conformity Accuracy* Integrity Timeliness Context	Integrity Timeliness Fit-fo- Purpose
How do you test for it?				
Build	Unit Functional (Regression)	Unit Functional (Regression)	Unit Functional (Regression)	Functional (Regression)
Automate	Integration Functional	Integration Functional	Integration Functional	Functional
Monitor	Performance Functional Conformity Completeness	Performance Functional -Conformity -Consistency -Accuracy -Integrity -Timeliness	Performance Functional -Conformity -Consistency -Accuracy -Integrity -Timeliness - Context	Performance

APPENDIX C

Reading List

This is a curated list of books that were recommended to me during my time researching this book. Some are obviously related to the topic of data governance, agile or IT, others are just great reads.

Sinek, Simon. *Start with why: how great leaders get everyone on the same page.* Penguin Group, 2009. Print

McKeown, Les. *Predictable Success: getting your organization on the growth track and keeping it there.* Greenleaf Book Group, LLC. 2010. Print.

Olson, Jack. *Data Quality: the accuracy dimension.* Morgan Kaufman. 2003. Print.

Dyche, Jill. *The New IT: How Technology Leaders are Enabling Business Strategy in the Digital Age.* McGraw-Hill Education, 2015. Print

Sebastian-Coleman, Laura. *Measuring Data Quality for Ongoing Improvement: A Data Quality Assessment Framework.* Morgan Kaufman. 2013. Print.

Kim, Gene; Humble, Jez; Debois, Patrick; Willis, John. *The DevOps Handbook: How to Create World-Class Agility, Reliability, and Security in Technology Organizations.* IT Revolution Press, 2016. Print.

Humble, Jez; Molesky, Joanne; O'Reilly, Barry. *The Lean Enterprise: How High Performance Organizations Scale.* O'Reilly Media, 2014.

Kim, Gene; Behr, Kevin; Spafford, George. *The Phoenix Project: A Novel about IT, DevOps, and Helping Your Business Win.* IT Revolution Press, 2018.

Lencioni, Patrick. *Overcoming the Five Dysfunctions of a Team: A Field Guide for Leaders, Managers, and Facilitators.* Jossey-Bass, 2005. Print

Keller, Gary; Papasan, Jay. *The ONE Thing: The Surprisingly Simple Truth Behind Extraordinary Results.* Bard Press, 2013. Print.

Nason, Rick. *It's Not Complicated: The Art and Science of Complexity in Business.* Rotman-UTP Publishing, 2017. Print.

Seiner, Robert. *Non-Invasive Data Governance: The Path of Least Resistance and Greatest Success.* Technics Publications, 2014. Print.

Bibliography

Chapter One

Sinek, Simon. *Start with why: how great leaders get everyone on the same page.* Penguin Group, 2009. Print.

Chapter Two

Stewardship. 2019. In *Merriam-Webster.com* retrieved January 11, 2019, from https://bit.ly/2lAfNdc.

"DataOps Manifesto" (August 12, 2019) retrieved from https://www.dataopsmanifesto.org/.

Chapter Three

Merrill, Douglas (2011, February 01). *And now for something completely different: context shifting.* Retrieved from https://bit.ly/2zuzgzV.

Chapter Four

Harmonized Data Quality Terminology and Framework, (2016) Kahn, et al eGEMS.

Underwood, Jen. (2017, August 30). *Why you need a data catalog and how to select one.* Retrieved from https://bit.ly/2jX4njn.

Schulze, Elizabeth. (2019, March 6). *40% of A.I. start-ups in Europe have almost nothing to do with A.I., research finds.* Retrieved from https://cnb.cx/2TqDioH.

Chapter Five

What is organizational culture? n.d. Retrieved from https://bit.ly/2KUq4Kr.

Diaz, Alejandro, Rowshankish, Kayvaun, Saleh, Tamim. (2018, September) McKinsey Quarterly. *Why Data Culture Matters.* Retrieved from https://mck.co/2wPN72R.

Stewart, Thomas A. (1994, February 7). *Rate your readiness to change.* Retrieved from https://cnn.it/2jUZqaM.

Babich, Nick. (2018, February 9). *Ten tips to develop better empathy maps* retrieved from https://adobe.ly/2Umc4Qe.

What is the ADKAR Model? n.d. Retrieved from https://bit.ly/1qKvLyJ.

Why Change Management? n.d. Retrieved from https://bit.ly/2PTdAUy.

Nason, Rick. *It's Not Complicated: The Art and Science of Complexity in Business*. Rotman-UTP Publishing, 2017. Print.

Chapter Six

Olson, Jack. *Data Quality: The Accuracy Dimension.* 2003. Morgan Kaufman.

Six dimensions of EHDI Data Quality Assessment. n.d. Retrieved from https://bit.ly/2UfxSut.

Quantifying the Effect of Data Quality on the Validity of an eMeasure Johnson et al. Appl Clin Inform 2017;8:1012–1021.

Chapter Seven

Mueller, Ernest (2019, January 12). *What is DevOps?* Retrieved from https://bit.ly/2aL34PV.

Index

Made in the USA
Monee, IL
30 December 2020

55960722R00105